Historic Homes of the American Presidents

SECOND, REVISED EDITION WITH 161 ILLUSTRATIONS

Irvin Haas

DOVER PUBLICATIONS, INC., *New York*

Publisher's Note, 1991

THIS GUIDE TO THE Presidents' homes has been extensively revised and updated for the second edition. Since the original publication of this book, many of the homes operated as museums have altered their interiors, in most cases visiting information has changed, and the Richard M. Nixon birthplace in Yorba Linda, California, has been opened to the public. In some instances new historical information has come to light. For this edition the text of this book has been thoroughly revised—and, where necessary, new photographs substituted for old—to reflect all of the above-mentioned developments. In addition, new chapters have been included on the homes of Presidents Ford, Carter, Reagan and Bush.

A reasonable attempt has been made to provide here the most up-to-date visiting information. Museum hours and admission charges, however, change frequently, and Dover Publications cannot be held responsible for any inconvenience caused by outdated information. In any case, it is advisable to telephone ahead for current information if a visit to any of the Presidents' homes is contemplated.

For our grandson
COLIN CAMPBELL CLODE

Copyright © 1976, 1991 by Irvin Haas.
All rights reserved under Pan American and International Copyright Conventions.

Published in Canada by General Publishing Company, Ltd., 30 Lesmill Road, Don Mills, Toronto, Ontario.
Published in the United Kingdom by Constable and Company, Ltd., 3 The Lanchesters, 162–164 Fulham Palace Road, London W6 9ER.

This Dover edition, first published in 1991, is a revised and enlarged republication of the work first published by the David McKay Company, Inc., New York, 1976. Details of the extent of the revisions and additions are furnished in the Publisher's Note.

Manufactured in the United States of America
Dover Publications, Inc., 31 East 2nd Street, Mineola, N.Y. 11501

Library of Congress Cataloging-in-Publication Data

Haas, Irvin.
    Historic homes of the American presidents / by Irvin Haas. — 2nd, rev. ed.
        p.   cm.
    Includes index.
    ISBN 0-486-26751-2
    1. Presidents—United States—Dwellings.   I. Title.
E159.H123   1991
973'.0992—dc20
    [B]   91-21782
                                                                                         CIP

Contents

Preface to the First Edition

A HOUSE IS A witness—silent, yet revealing.

Even as it stands discreetly mute about the innumerable privacies it has seen and heard, it emanates a kind of testimony—some of it profoundly enlightening, some of it tantalizingly suggestive—about those whom it sheltered.

Each mirror at Versailles, each gold clock in the royal palace at Madrid, each jewel, painting, tapestry, porcelain and article of enormous wealth displayed in all the magnificent castles and palaces of the old world—now peopled only by tourists and security guards—bears witness to those who once lived there. The monumentality of the architecture and the immensity of the wealth testify to the awe demanded of the ruled for the ruler. They speak of the tastes and values of the imperial sovereigns, not in the detached way of words but in the engaging power of the actual. These structures and the things they contain are limited witnesses, to be sure, but also fascinating ones. They withhold far, far more than they tell, but they do give us a haunting sense—a feeling rather than a knowing—of what it was like when these rooms were animated by those for whom they were built. A whiff of the past.

Just as evocative—but of far different people in a far different place—are the homes of our Presidents. The very diversity of these structures—from huts to mansions—attests to the diversity that is a hallmark of our national character. They reveal how democratic we have been in opening the door to the highest office in the land to leaders rising out of all walks of life.

A tour of these buildings, of course, offers us an interesting survey of American architectural styles as well as a fascinating picture of what life and people were like at different times in different places. But the deepest value of a visit to these houses lies in what they tell us of the origins and character of the men who lived there— rustic and aristocrat, businessman and scholar, soldier and preacher, lawyer and layman—who led us through our first two centuries as a nation.

Lincoln's log-cabin birthplace, the vitality of its story frozen in myth, deserves to be seen so that we can get a hint of the real life to which it was witness. Here is testimony to the courage and perseverance of those who made this land, testimony to the greatness that could rise out of a mean and lonely place where survival, let alone growing up to become a great and wise national leader, was a wondrous accomplishment. No wonder the myth has taken over.

And just as the primitive cabin tells us so much about Lincoln, so does a sophisticated Monticello tell us so much about Jefferson. To desire, design and build such a home reveals the taste, intellect and ability of a man so prominent among those who desired, designed and built such a new nation.

This book is a tourist's guide to that humble hut, that elegant mansion and all the other birthplaces and homes of our Presidents accessible to public inspection. A tour of these homes is a journey through a varied gallery of Americana. From the banal to the beautiful, these homes, with their furnishings, their paintings, their artifacts, speak much about their times and of those men who made such special impressions on those times.

Not every home of every President is included in this book because many of those homes no longer exist and because others, owned privately, are not open to public inspection. What is included, along with brief biographical sketches, are pictures and information about fifty-three homes associated with thirty-six of our Presidents. Most are open to the public. The range of sites is wide—from such marvelously preserved architectural and historical treasures as Mount Vernon and Monticello, the Hermitage and Wheatland, to the pathetic little replicas of the cabin birthplace of Millard Fillmore and childhood home of Chester Alan Arthur, whose later homes have long since disappeared.

There is no chapter about William McKinley, Jr., for example, because there is no longer any house. The original site of his birthplace was in Niles, Ohio. Years later the building was moved to the rear of its original site and used as an undertaker's storehouse. It was extensively vandalized in 1909, spurring a restoration project. The house was moved to McKinley Heights in Niles, where it was used as a McKinley museum. In 1934 this restored house caught fire and its contents were destroyed. Considered beyond repair, the structure was razed.

Several other homes, on the other hand, are in fine shape, but inaccessible to the public because they are still in private hands. Oak Hill, for example, the home of James Monroe, in Loudoun County, Virginia, is one of the most impressive of these. This stately red brick mansion, designed by Thomas Jefferson and James Hoban, the original architect of the White House, is a treasure, owned, occupied and maintained with tender loving care by Mrs. Thomas N. DeLashmott. Others not open to the public and not included in this book are: Montpelier, home of James Madison, in Orange County, Virginia, privately owned and occupied; and Westland, at Princeton, New Jersey, home of Grover Cleveland, a private home occupied by Mrs. J. Taylor Woodward.

I regret these omissions forced on us by the ravages of time and the tyrannies of circumstance. What follows is an introduction and guide to all those Presidential buildings that are accessible. I hope that a tour through these pages will in some small way stimulate and enhance your visit to the real thing.

IRVIN HAAS

1

The White House

HOME OF THE PRESIDENTS, WASHINGTON, D.C.

HOW TO GET THERE/WHEN TO VISIT

The White House is located in the District of Columbia at 1600 Pennsylvania Avenue, N.W., opposite Lafayette Square in downtown Washington. It is open to the public for tours Tuesday through Saturday, from 10 A.M. to 12 noon. There is no charge for the tour; however, during the summer season (Memorial Day to Labor Day), tickets must be obtained. These are distributed each day on the Ellipse beginning at 8 A.M., on a first-come, first-served basis. Tel.: (202) 456–7041 or 472–3669.

THE WHITE HOUSE HAS been the official residence of our nation's Presidents since 1800, late in the administration of our second President, John Adams. As a national shrine symbolizing the honor and dignity of the highest office in the land, it has been the scene of many historic events and brilliant social affairs. Like the nation itself, it bears the influence of successive chief executives. Although rebuilt and modernized, it retains the simplicity, charm and dignity of the original structure.

President George Washington approved the plans for the White House drawn by the Irish-born James Hoban, who had won the prize competition planned by the Commissioners of the Federal city. The mansion and the Capitol were the first public buildings erected in the Federal city. The cornerstone was laid on October 13, 1792. Workmen used light gray sandstone from the Aquia Creek quarry in Virginia for the exterior walls of both buildings. During the course of construction or soon thereafter, workmen painted them white. The building was thus unofficially termed the "White House" from an early date, although for many years it was usually referred to as the "President's House," or the "President's Palace."

The main façade of the White House, in the Georgian style, resembles the Duke of Leinster's mansion in Dublin. Hoban probably derived the details of other faces and the interior arrangement from various British and European mansions. He supervised the original construction, the rebuilding after the burning by the British in 1814 and the erection of the north and south porticoes some years later. Over the

The White House, built in 1792–99 in the Georgian style of gray sandstone and painted white as early as 1798. Shown is the main or north entrance. The large portico that covers the entrance and driveway was added in 1829. The President and his family use the south entrance, which is completely covered.

years other architects, notably Benjamin Latrobe during and after the Jefferson administration, modified Hoban's original plans.

President and Mrs. John Adams were the first occupants, in November 1800, when the government moved from Philadelphia to Washington. Some of the interior had not yet been completed, and Mrs. Adams used the unfinished East Room to dry the family wash. During Jefferson's administration the east and west terraces were constructed. Jefferson opened the mansion each morning to all arrivals. In 1809, when James Madison became President, his wife, Dolley, introduced some of the brilliance and glitter of Old World courts into the social life of the White House.

In August 1814, during the War of 1812, British forces captured the city and set fire to the White House, the Capitol and other government buildings in retaliation for the destruction by U.S. troops of some public buildings in Canada. Before Mrs. Madison fled to refuge in the Dunbarton House in Georgetown, she managed to remove many valuable documents and the Gilbert Stuart portrait of George Washington that now hangs in the East Room. Only the partially damaged exterior walls and interior brickwork remained when reconstruction began in the spring of 1815. The Madisons lived out his term of office in the Octagon House and one of the "Seven Buildings," a group of buildings located on the corner of 19th Street and Pennsylvania Avenue. In December 1817 the newly elected President, James Monroe, was able to occupy the White House. The south portico, the dominant architectural feature on that side, was added in 1824, and the large north portico over the entrance and the driveway was built in 1829.

Although the White House has since been extensively renovated and modernized, the old sandstone walls have been preserved. The aim has been to retain the original atmosphere while at the same time providing a more livable home for the President and his family. Furnishings and decorations on the first floor are predominantly in 19th- and early 20th-century styles. Portraits of several Presidents and First Ladies hang in the lobby, main corridor and rooms on the first floor. Six classic columns separate the lobby from the main corridor. The columns and pilasters spaced along the walls are of varicolored Vermont marble; the floors are of gray and pink Tennessee marble. The seals of the thirteen original states are carved on the marble-faced opening of the stairway.

Located on the first floor are the East Room, the Green Room, the Blue Room, the Red Room, the State Dining Room and the Family Dining Room. The East Room, the largest in the White House, is used for state receptions and balls. It has been the scene of several weddings, including those of Nelly Grant and Alice Roosevelt, as well as the funeral services for Presidents William Henry Harrison, Zachary Taylor, Abraham Lincoln, Warren G. Harding and Franklin D. Roosevelt. The bodies of Presidents William McKinley and John F. Kennedy lay in repose in this room. On the east wall is the most notable portrait in the White House: Gilbert Stuart's full-length study of George Washington.

The Green Room, used for informal receptions, has been restored as a Federal parlor of about 1800–1815. The furniture is of American design, based on English styles.

The Blue Room, known for its elliptical shape, is usually considered the most beautiful in the building. Portraits of the first seven Presidents hang in this room, where the President receives guests at state dinners and receptions. It has been redecorated to represent the period of President Monroe. Grover Cleveland and Frances Folsom were married in this room in 1886, the only wedding of a President to take place in the White House.

The Red Room, completely redecorated in 1961 as an American Empire parlor, is used as an informal reception room by the First Lady. In March 1877 Rutherford B. Hayes took his oath of office in this room. Among the furnishings is a sofa that once belonged to Dolley Madison and Nelly Custis.

The East Room, used for balls and as a reception room on state occasions. It has been the scene of various weddings and funerals, and the bodies of Presidents McKinley and Kennedy lay in repose here.

Another view of the East Room.

Exceeded in size only by the East Room, the State Dining Room can easily accommodate a hundred guests at large dinners or luncheons. The Family Dining Room was refurnished in 1961 in the early-19th-century style.

The second and third floors are reserved for the Presidential family and guests. The Lincoln Bedroom, in which stands a massive, eight-foot bed purchased for guests by Mrs. Lincoln, is furnished in the Victorian style. The adjoining room—the Cabinet Room from about 1865 to 1902, later the Treaty Room—is now used as a private office by the President. The Rose Guest Room (Queen's Bedroom) is furnished as an elegant lady's bedchamber of the early 19th century.

A corridor with vaulted ceiling and varicolored Vermont marble walls leads to the rooms on the ground floor. The China Room, Library and Vermeil Room are paneled in pine recovered from the old beams of the White House. The oval Diplomatic Reception Room was furnished in 1960 with neoclassical furniture and

The former Treaty Room (before that the Cabinet Room) on the second floor as it appeared a number of years ago. Since this photograph was taken, the room has been redecorated.

a rug with seals of the fifty states. The Library, redesigned in 1961–62, contains a suite of rare Duncan Phyfe furniture. In 1952 the original kitchen, equipped with the old sandstone fireplaces, was restored. Adjoining it is a modern electric kitchen.

The simple dignity of the White House is enhanced by the natural beauty of its informal but beautifully landscaped grounds. Many of the trees and shrubs are of historical interest, such as the magnolias planted by President Andrew Jackson.

2

George Washington

THE BIRTHPLACE SITE NEAR FREDERICKSBURG, VIRGINIA; AND MOUNT VERNON, IN VIRGINIA.

HOW TO GET THERE/WHEN TO VISIT

George Washington Birthplace National Monument is on the Potomac River, 38 miles east of Fredericksburg, Virginia, with access from Va. 3 via Va. 204. The site is open every day except December 25 and January 1 from 9 A.M. to 5 P.M. The admission fee is $1 for persons 17 to 61 years of age; all others free. Tel.: (804) 224–1732.

Mount Vernon is located at the end of the George Washington Memorial Parkway, eight miles south of Alexandria, Virginia, and 16 miles from downtown Washington, D.C. From mid-March to October, Spirit of Washington operates boat service out of Washington to the site. Mount Vernon is open to the public every day in the year from 9 A.M. to 5 P.M. (March 1 to October 31) or to 4 P.M. (November 1 to the last day of February). Adults pay $6 admission; special rates available for seniors, children, students and groups. Tel.: (703) 780–2000.

THE SECOND OFFICER OF an English merchant ship that had foundered in the Potomac River during a storm left the ship after she was refloated early in 1657. A year later he married Anne Pope, daughter of Colonel Nathaniel Pope, a leading planter of the area. The young officer was John Washington, destined to be the great-grandfather of President George Washington.

After the wedding the bride's father gave the couple 700 acres of land as a wedding gift. In 1664 John moved his family to a new house on Bridges Creek, four miles east of Mattox Creek.

John Washington prospered. He took an active interest in public affairs, served in numerous civil offices including the Virginia House of Burgesses, led a military expedition against the Indians and rose to such prominence that the name of the local Anglican parish was changed to Washington in his honor. Here his son Lawrence prospered, following his father in the House of Burgesses and serving in local offices both civil and martial.

The Memorial House near Fredericksburg, Virginia, constructed in 1930–31 to resemble a typical home of the period of Washington's birth. The bricks are made from local clay.

Lawrence's son Augustine continued this tradition of public service as he developed his own estate. In 1718 he purchased from the Abbington family two tracts, totaling 200 acres, on Popes Creek about one mile east of his Bridges Creek home. Here, between 1722 and 1726, he most likely enlarged the house that became the birthplace of the first President of the United States. Augustine's first wife, Jane Butler, died in 1729, leaving him with three small children. He married again, this time Mary Ball, the daughter of Colonel Joseph Ball of Epping Forest. The first of their children was born on February 22, 1732. He was named George.

Young George Washington spent the first three and one-half years of his life at the Popes Creek Plantation. In 1735 his father moved the family to Little Hunting Creek Plantation, later known as Mount Vernon. After four years, Augustine, for business reasons, moved the family to Ferry Farm on the Rappahannock River near Fredericksburg. There, when George was eleven, his father died.

George's half-brother, Augustine, Jr., inherited the Popes Creek Plantation where, from time to time during the ensuing years, young George lived and grew very close to Augustine.

Popes Creek Plantation was a lively, functioning farm. The impressions young George gathered there from the many farm activities stayed with him all his life, forming the background for his own activities at his beloved Mount Vernon.

On Christmas Day, 1779, while General George Washington was leading the Continental Army in the fight for American independence, his birthplace accidently caught fire and burned. George's half-nephew, William Augustine Washington, who was then master of the plantation, moved his family to another home several miles away. The birthplace was never rebuilt. For thirty-six years the site lay unattended, until George Washington Parke Custis, General Washington's adopted son, marked it with a stone tablet. As the years passed, this tablet, as well as whatever vestiges remained of the original birthplace and its out-buildings, disappeared.

In 1858 the Commonwealth of Virginia acquired the sites of the home and the nearby burying ground, but the Civil War ended any immediate plans to mark the site. In 1882 the land was donated by Virginia to the Federal government, and fourteen years later a granite shaft was erected on the site to the memory of George Washington.

In 1923 the Wakefield National Memorial Association was formed to recover and restore the birthplace grounds. The association brought the holding to 394 acres. In 1930–31 a Memorial House and kitchen were built and furnished, and a colonial garden was established. In 1932, the year of the two hundredth anniversary of George Washington's birth, the park was officially opened and title transferred to the Federal government. The Colonial Farm was established in 1968.

On the actual birthplace site, the foundations, which have been covered by earth for preservation, are those of the main house of the plantation, the building in which George was born. It was a sizable, **U**-shaped building of at least nine rooms. The foundation outline is marked with crushed oystershell today.

Dining room in the Memorial House, George Washington Birthplace National Monument. Most of the furnishings are more than two hundred years old.

Children's room and master bedroom at the George Washington Birthplace National Monument. (Photographs by Walter H. Miller.)

Kitchen, built on the site of the original kitchen at Popes Creek Plantation. In Washington's time the kitchen was a separate building in order to minimize the risk of fire and to keep excessive heat and odors out of the main house.

The Memorial House represents a typical home of the period, with four rooms and a central hallway on each floor. The bricks were handmade from the clay of an adjoining field. A small table in the parlor is believed to have been in the original house, and most of the other furnishings are more than two hundred years old. The house and furnishings illustrate the environment into which Washington was born and the manner of life that his father led as a moderately wealthy planter in 18th-century tidewater Virginia.

The kitchen of the Popes Creek Plantation was located in a separate building, a common practice to avoid the danger of fire and the discomfort from the excessive heat and odors generated in cooking. The present structure, which occupies the site of the original kitchen, has been furnished as a typical 18th-century kitchen.

The present Colonial Living Farm re-creates some of the scenes of farm life that were a major part of young George Washington's environment. The livestock, poultry and crops are of old varieties and are raised by methods that were common during the Colonial period. The smells, sights and sounds that greet you are the same that greeted young George as he roamed through the area.

Burnt House Point is an eighty-year-old grove of cedars which affords excellent views of Popes Creek and the waterfowl of the area. The creek leads to the Potomac River, which linked the Colonial plantations to the outside world. It was a lifeline for supplies and an essential route for marketing cash crops. The activity at the wharf marked a high point in the lives of everyone on the plantation.

When John Washington, George's great-grandfather, settled in the Bridges Creek area, he established nearby a family burying ground where many of the Washingtons were interred. Evidence has been found of thirty-two burials at this location, including those of George's half-brother, father, grandfather and great-grandfather.

East front of the mansion at Mount Vernon, built by Augustine Washington, George's father, and expanded by George Washington. Believed to be his own architect, Washington added the columned piazza that extends the length of the east front, an innovation in its day. (Courtesy The Mount Vernon Ladies' Assocation.)

Two of the original gravestones are replicated and five memorial tablets were placed here in the 1930s to honor the American ancestors of our first President.

In 1793 George Washington wrote to an English correspondent:

No estate in United America is more pleasantly situated than this [Mount Vernon]. It lies in a high, dry and healthy Country 300 miles by water from the Sea . . . on one of the finest Rivers in the World. . . . It is situated in a latitude between the extremes of heat and cold, and is the same distance by land and water, with good roads and the best navigation [to and] from the Federal City, Alexandria and George town; distant from the first twelve, from the second nine, and from the last sixteen miles.

Time has not changed Washington's description of the grounds. They remain largely as he planted them late in the 18th century. Mount Vernon stands as a monument "pleasantly situated" on a commanding eminence, overlooking the

Potomac and the low Maryland hills. The tree-crowded hilltop, the wide sweep of the river, and the wooded shores beyond present a view of unchanging beauty, one of the best remaining examples of the plantations around which the highly developed social and economic life of the 18th-century South centered.

The estate's history began in 1674, when John Washington, great-grandfather of George, patented the Mount Vernon homesite. In 1726, Augustine, father of George, acquired the property from his sister Mildred; he lived there with his young family from 1735 to 1738. In 1743, Augustine Washington died, and Lawrence Washington, George's elder half-brother, married and settled at Mount Vernon. In 1752 Lawrence died, and two years later George Washington officially acquired Mount Vernon by release from Lawrence's widow.

From 1752 until 1759, because of his military service as aide to General Braddock and as commander of the Virginia militia, George Washington was seldom able to visit Mount Vernon. During this period the plantation was managed by his younger brother, John Augustine. In late 1758 George Washington returned to private life, and in January 1759 married Martha Dandridge Custis, widow of Daniel Parke Custis. Washington envisaged an ideal retirement. To an English friend he wrote, "I am now, I believe, fixed at this Seat with an agreeable Consort for Life and hope to find more happiness in retirement than I ever experienced amidst a wide and bustling World." He was to be disappointed in his expectations of retirement, but the peaceful years with Martha at Mount Vernon before the Revolution were the happiest of their lives. In 1775 he was appointed commander-in-chief of the Continental Army and left for New England. He was to stop again at Mount Vernon only briefly en route to and from Yorktown in 1781. In 1783 he resigned his commission and returned to his home hoping once again to savor the good life at Mount Vernon, but once again he was to be disappointed. He assumed the Presidency in 1789, and in the eight years of his term he visited Mount Vernon just fifteen times, remaining for periods which varied from several days to several months. On his retirement in March 1797, he returned home once again, and for the two and a half years that remained to him, he enjoyed the tranquility he had so long desired.

In the forty-five years of George Washington's tenure, Mount Vernon grew from 2,126 acres to more than 8,000. By the terms of his will the estate was divided after the death of Mrs. Washington in 1802. The Mansion House and 4,000 acres were bequeathed to his nephew Bushrod, son of John Augustine Washington. To his grandnephews, George Fayette Washington and Charles Augustine Washington, he bequeathed the River Farm, a tract of over 2,000 acres north of Little Hunting Creek. To his nephew Lawrence Lewis and his wife, Eleanor, granddaughter of Mrs. Washington, he bequeathed about 2,000 acres on both sides of Dogue Creek, including the mill. On a commanding site overlooking the creek, the young couple built Woodlawn, a fine Georgian home that is open to the public in a restored state. The mill has also been reconstructed and is open to the public.

The more than 8,000 acres of Mount Vernon were divided into five farms, each a complete unit, with its overseer, workers, livestock, equipment and buildings. The four outlying farms were highly developed and well cultivated. The brick barns on several of the farms were finer than many of those built during that period in America. One, a sixteen-sided structure designed by George Washington, had a unique threshing floor in the loft. It was George's custom, when in residence, to ride daily about his farms, inspecting, planning and directing. Despite the major diversions of his public service, Washington was one of the most progressive farmers of his day, turning early to crop rotation and soil conservation.

The outlying farms no longer exist. The Mansion House Farm was not a farm in the usual sense but a manor house developed as a gentleman's country seat. When the mansion was first acquired by George after the death of his brother, it was of a modest size and typical of its period and locale. Built by his father, it was one and a half stories high, with a central hall and four small rooms on the first floor. Between 1754 and 1799, George, believed to be his own architect, developed Mount Vernon into one of the finest estates of its time. The modest house was more than doubled in size, and successfully incorporated many of the architectural refinements then so popular in England. The most striking architectural feature of the mansion is the high-columned piazza, extending the full length of the house, an excellent adaptation of design to setting and climate. It was an innovation that entitles George Washington to distinction among architects.

The exterior finish of the mansion and the courtyard dependencies is another unusual feature. The siding was beveled to give an appearance of stone; sand was then applied to the freshly painted surface. Washington called this "rusticated boards."

The showpiece of the mansion is the large dining room, most frequently designated in Washington's writings as "the New Room." This was an addition to the original house and one that preoccupied Washington even in 1776, when he was menaced by the British army. He sent plans for the room stating "the chimney of the new room should be exactly in the middle of it—the doors and everything else to be exactly answerable and uniform—in short I would have the whole executed in a

The large dining room at Mount Vernon, added to the original house by George Washington. Shown here is the south wall, with the original elegant marble mantelpiece and vases sent to George Washington by Samuel Vaughan in 1785. (Courtesy The Mount Vernon Ladies' Association.)

A corner of the west parlor, showing Martha Washington's tea service and a copy of the first known portrait of George Washington, painted by Charles Willson Peale in 1772. (Courtesy The Mount Vernon Ladies' Association.)

masterly manner." The room interior remained unfinished until several years after the war while he sought a craftsman who could execute the decoration of ceiling and woodwork in a manner equal to his expectations. His correspondence expressed a preference for plain wallpaper, green or blue, with harmonizing border. The green of the present paper and the detail of the border are derived from scraps of the originals. From Philadelphia in 1787 he directed that the woodwork of the room be painted a buff color. This letter and the physical evidence of partial modification later have determined the woodwork colors as now restored. In January 1799 a young English guest noted "white chintz window curtains with deep festoons of green satin" in the room. The present draping of the windows, incorporating satin and dimity of proper color and weave, follows the fashion of the period.

The mantel and its vases were gifts of Samuel Vaughan, an English admiral and friend of Washington. They arrived in 1785. Outstanding among the furnishings of this room is the pair of Hepplewhite sideboards. The the right of the Palladian window is the surviving mate of a pair made in 1797 for this room by John Aitken of Philadelphia. The matching period sideboard was provided to restore the balance of the room. The large gilt looking glasses and the row of identical chairs were also provided by Aitken.

Two 18th-century landscape painters—George Beck and William Winstanley—

are represented by four large oils personally selected by George Washington. There are also other paintings and engravings, including the Trumbull engravings of *The Death of General Montgomery* and *The Battle of Bunker's Hill.*

The central hall, or "passage," extends the full width of the house from the front door on the courtyard side of the piazza overlooking the river. During the warm season it was the most comfortable room in the house. Between the doorways to the downstairs bedroom and the dining room hangs a key of the Bastille, a gift from General Lafayette transmitted by Thomas Paine. Over the double doors leading to the piazza are two plaster lions received from England in 1760.

The "Little Parlor" is the music room containing the harpsichord imported from London by Washington for his granddaughter, Nelly Custis. On the harpsichord is a bound volume of the music she played.

The prints over the harpsichord are duplicates of marine scenes listed in this room by Washington's executors. The Windsor chairs are not original. The chair cushions are reproductions of originals made by Mrs. Washington for her own Windsor chairs. The carpeting is a reproduction of the type used in the mansion.

Architecturally, the west parlor, which dates from the first enlargement of the house, is one of the most interesting rooms in the mansion. The decorated ceiling of Adamesque design, the door frames, the paneled walls and the splendid mantel combine to make it one of the finest surviving examples of Colonial Virginia interiors. In the pediment over the mantel is a carved and painted representation of the Washington family coat of arms, which also appears in a decorative panel at the top of an original mirror that hangs between the windows of the room. A variant is cast in the iron fireback of the fireplace opening, one of four purchased in Philadelphia in 1787. Originally the more important family pictures hung in this room. Today, several portraits that were in this room during Washington's life are in position again, including a copy of a Charles Willson Peale portrait of him. There are a number of original objects in the room, including urn-shaped silver lamps and a china tea set.

The family dining room has an ornate mantel and decorated ceiling, executed in 1775. There are many pictures on its walls. While the mahogany dining room is original, the table setting is a replica based on a contemporary description. The English sideboard table approximates the original. There are nine original side chairs (Chippendale ladder-back type). Other originals include the andirons, wine chest, two small tables, and the mirror hanging between the windows.

The downstairs bedroom was a common feature of early Virginia homes, as there was always a need for an extra sleeping chamber to accommodate unexpected guests. This room continued to serve as a bedroom until the end of Washington's life. There are five bedchambers on the second floor in addition to the master's sleeping quarters over the library. There are fewer noteworthy objects in these chambers than in the rooms on the lower floor, but a few deserve notice. In the corner of the Lafayette Bedroom is the trunk Mrs. Washington took on her journeys. In the Nelly Custis Bedroom is a crib given to Nelly by her grandmother, Martha Washington, for Nelly's first child.

There are seven rooms on the third floor, two of which are furnished as bedrooms to provide for visitors who could not be accommodated on the floors below. The remaining rooms are "lumber rooms," an 18th-century term for storerooms.

The General and Mrs. Washington's bedchamber constitutes the second floor of the south addition to the mansion. A narrow stairway from the floor below gave them a measure of privacy. In this room and on the bed there, George Washington died on December 14, 1799. The present bed hangings were reproduced from a fragment of original Mount Vernon dimity. Mrs. Washington's writing desk and dressing table are along the west wall. Most of the other objects in the room are identified as Mount Vernon memorabilia, including the lacquered dressing glass and the five prints in round frames.

The study was an important feature of the enlarged mansion. The addition at the south end, of which this room is a part, had been enclosed under Washington's direction before he departed to attend the Second Continental Congress in May 1775. The study interior was finished under the direction of his manager, Lund Washington. The bookcases were not installed until some years later. This room, the headquarters from which George Washington ran his estate, is the one most intimately associated with his life at Mount Vernon. As "the focus of political intelligence for the new world," no private chamber in the land has more fruitful associations with great events. At the close of his Presidency, he purchased the secretary-desk. The accompanying chair; the bookcase standing between the windows, purchased in Philadelphia in 1798; and the terrestrial globe standing near the window are all original pieces. There is also a small table on which the Washingtons had their wedding breakfast at the home of the bride. A replica of Houdon's bust of John Paul Jones is here, along with a copy of Houdon's famous bust of George Washington (the original may be viewed in the museum). The original library consisted of 884 bound volumes. Ninety of the original volumes have been acquired by gift and purchase, and more than three hundred are represented by duplicates. The pantry contains some original blue-and-white Canton china.

Approximately a dozen buildings are open for public inspection. These include the kitchen and storehouse and the servant's hall, which also housed the resident shoemaker and tailor. The gardener's house was used by overseers and storekeepers and was the depository from which tools and materials were issued. The museum, a modern structure built in 1928, houses a growing collection of Washington memorabilia, including swords, military sashes, china, textiles, silver plate and miniatures. The brick stable at the foot of the south lane was built in 1782 and houses a unique two-wheeled riding chair and a coach purchased by Mrs. Washington's grandson.

Finally, one may make a pilgrimage to the tomb at the foot of the vineyard, where on a stone tablet above the vault gate appears this inscription: "Within this Enclosure Rest the remains of Genl. George Washington."

3

John Adams and Son

THE BIRTHPLACES OF JOHN ADAMS AND JOHN QUINCY ADAMS;
AND THE FAMILY HOME, "THE OLD HOUSE,"
IN QUINCY, MASSACHUSETTS.

HOW TO GET THERE/WHEN TO VISIT

All three of these dwellings are in Quincy, Massachusetts, about 8 miles
south of Boston, and can be reached via the S.E. Expressway, Exit 8. The
John Adams birthplace is located at 133 Franklin Street, and the **John
Quincy Adams birthplace** is at 141 Franklin. Both are open to visitors daily
from 9 A.M. to 5 P.M. from April 19 to November 10. Admission $2 (pass good
for 7 days; includes "The Old House"). Those 16 and under, free. Tel.: (617)
773-1177.

"The Old House" (The Adams National Historic Site) is located at 135
Adams Street, at Newport Avenue and Furnace Brook Parkway, one block
west of Hancock Street. Open daily from 9 A.M. to 5 P.M. from April 19 to
November 10. Admission: see above.

THE BIRTHPLACES OF PRESIDENTS John and John Quincy Adams stand in the city
of Quincy, Massachusetts, on the old coast road from Boston to Plymouth. Known
as the Country Highway, this road was ordered laid out by the General Court in
1640 in what was known until 1792 as the town of Braintree.

John Adams, first Vice-President and second President of the United States, was
born on October 19, 1735, graduated from Harvard College in 1755, and was
admitted to the bar in 1758. He took a keen interest in town affairs and wrote on
public matters for the newspapers. In 1764 he married Abigail, daughter of the
Reverend William and Elizabeth (Quincy) Smith of Weymouth, Massachusetts.
Abigail was a remarkable woman, a tower of strength to her husband. Her lively
letters give wonderful pictures of those exciting times—from domestic concerns to
the Battle of Bunker Hill. She is the only woman who has been the wife of one of our
Presidents and the mother of another.

Active against the Stamp Act and an early supporter of the patriotic cause, John Adams was chosen one of the delegates from Massachusetts to the First Continental Congress. After fighting began at Lexington, he took a leading part in the Second Continental Congress, headed the movement for independence, and was largely responsible for the choice of George Washington as Commander in Chief of the army. As one of the Committee of Five chosen to draft the Declaration of Independence, he was, in Jefferson's words, "the pillar of its support on the floor of Congress." After Burgoyne's surrender at Saratoga he was chosen commissioner to France and, with his ten-year-old son, John Quincy, sailed for Europe in February 1778. Later he was commissioned minister plenipotentiary to Holland and succeeded in securing loans from that country. With Franklin and Jay, on September 3, 1783, he signed the peace treaty with Great Britain that brought independence to the United States. In 1785 he was appointed envoy to the Court of St. James, where he remained until 1788. With Franklin and Jefferson he selected *E Pluribus Unum* as the motto on the seal of the United States. In the new government under the Constitution he was elected Vice-President, and during both of Washington's terms he presided over the U.S. Senate. Elected President in 1796, Adams served with great ability and, fortunately for the country and despite the clamor of many of the leaders of his own party, prevented a war with France. In 1801 he retired to his home in Quincy but retained his deep interest in public questions, as is attested by his voluminous correspondence. He lived to see his son, John Quincy, elected to the Presidency, and died on July 4, 1826, the same day as Thomas Jefferson.

John Quincy Adams, born on July 11, 1767, from childhood gained an extraordinary knowledge of Europe. During his father's ministry to Great Britain, he returned to America to attend Harvard College, graduating in 1787. In 1794 Washington commissioned him minister to the Netherlands, and during his father's Presidency he was minister to Prussia. In 1803 he was elected to the U.S. Senate. Under President Madison he became, in 1809, minister to Russia, where he established friendly terms with Tsar Alexander. He refused nomination to the U.S. Supreme Court and remained in Europe as one of the peace commissioners who, on December 24, 1814, signed the Treaty of Ghent, which ended the war of 1812. He was in Paris in 1815 to witness Napoleon's triumphal return from Elba, the prelude to Waterloo. Adams next went to England as minister to the Court of St. James. In 1817 he became President Monroe's Secretary of State, negotiating with Spain for the cession of the Floridas. He took a prominent part in the recognition of the Latin American republics. Declaring that "the American continents are no longer subjects for any new European colonial establishments," Adams was jointly responsible with the President for the promulgation of the Monroe Doctrine.

In 1825 Adams took the oath of office as sixth President of the United States, serving until 1829, when he retired to Quincy, where he planned to write history. Within two years, however, he was elected to Congress and served continuously for seventeen years. He was the only President to become a member of the House of Representatives after a term in the White House. On February 21, 1848, at the age of eighty-one, he was stricken on the floor of the House and died at his post.

The John Adams birthplace at 133 Franklin Street originally consisted of two lower rooms and two chambers, with a massive central chimney. It was almost doubled at an early date by the addition of a lean-to, providing two more rooms on the ground floor and two small chambers at each end of the gable with a large attic space between. The huge fireplace in the east room marks the original kitchen. In the front entry is a door, leading to the cellar, with a typical 17th-century moulding; a gift of Mr. Samuel T. Crosby, it was brought to this house, after the latter's restoration, from the General Benjamin Lincoln House in Hingham.

Left: John Quincy Adams's birthplace, the salt-box farmhouse where John Adams lived with his wife, Abigail, in the 1760s and practiced law. Right: John Adams's birthplace. (Photograph by Oberg.)

A large barn and outbuildings which appear in old photographs were removed after farming ceased in the 1880s; a split-rail fence along the roads, since renewed, is a reminder of the original property boundaries.

The John Quincy Adams birthplace at 141 Franklin Street is a salt-box, originally consisting of two lower rooms and two chambers. Upon the addition of a lean-to in the rear a new fireplace and chimney stack were built for a new kitchen.

The former kitchen with its large fireplace was used by John Adams for his law office. A door at the corner by the street was added for the use of his clients; it was later boarded over, but it was found when the house was restored in 1896. In the fall of 1779, as a delegate to the convention that framed a constitution for Massachusetts, John Adams was instructed to draw up a draft for its consideration. This was done in the law office here, but Adams left for Europe before completing it.

On the second floor, in the north bedroom, where John Quincy Adams was born, the floor boards, more than two feet wide, are believed to be from timber cut on the farm. The south bedroom, that of John Quincy Adams, contains a large closet where he kept his library.

In places some of the original brick filling in the walls has been left exposed to show the construction. There are also patches showing the handmade laths and nails. By the back stairway, some of the original clapboards, with the old-style lap joints and some early plastering still in place, can be seen. The original beams supporting the first floor had to be replaced in 1950.

The house on Adams Street was first named "Peacefield" by John Adams but was later known in the family as the "Old House." It was very dear and close to them all.

The oldest part of the house was built in 1731 by Major Leonard Vassall, a wealthy West Indian sugar planter who had come to Massachusetts the year before. The house then consisted of only a paneled room, west entry and dining room on the ground floor; two bedrooms on the second floor; and three smaller rooms in the attic. The kitchen and servants' quarters were not attached to the house.

John Adams, while still minister to Great Britain, bought the house in September 1787 from the major's grandson, Leonard Vassall Borland, and on his return in 1788 took possession of the property. During his Presidency, Adams built the large gabled ell containing the long room, east entry and upstairs entry. In 1836 John Quincy Adams added the passage along the north side of the house containing the two ells. In 1869, Charles Francis Adams added thirty feet to the kitchen ell for servants' quarters, and the following year built the stone library overlooking his grandmother's garden. In 1873 he built the large stone carriage house. The present gates were added by Brooks Adams in 1906.

After his retirement from the Presidency in 1801, John Adams lived in the house year round until his death in 1826. John Quincy Adams and Charles Francis Adams made it their summer home. Much of the furniture reflects the diplomatic backgrounds of John, John Quincy and Charles Francis Adams, since each came back with possessions from their various European missions. The continuity of life in the house is best shown by the furnishings, with each generation contributing something of itself. The house is not a "period piece" but a house which, from 1788 to 1927, clearly shows the ever-changing style and taste of its occupants.

On its west side is an early-18th-century garden. The flowerbeds were planted by Mrs. Charles Francis Adams about 1850. In the northeast corner of the garden is the stone library, a separate building used by the third and fourth generation of Adamses. Books belonging to both Presidents, John and John Quincy, are on the shelves.

The "Old House" in Quincy, Massachusetts, purchased in 1787 by John Adams while minister to Great Britain. It is now part of the Adams National Historic Site, presented by the Adams family in 1946 to the United States government for the American people. The home, which was very dear to the family, contains priceless heirlooms and fine examples of Colonial furniture and furnishings, contributed by four successive generations of Adamses. The site also includes a garden, a stone library and a carriage house. (Photograph by Oberg.)

4

Thomas Jefferson

MONTICELLO AT CHARLOTTESVILLE, VIRGINIA.

HOW TO GET THERE/WHEN TO VISIT

Monticello can be reached by Interstate 64. Exit at Route 20 South, proceeding about 200 yards to the left turn for Monticello. Follow Route 53 for 2 miles to the entrance. It is open every day of the year except December 25. From March 1 to October 31 it is open from 8 A.M. to 5 P.M. From November 1 to the last day of February it is open from 9 A.M. to 4:30 P.M. Adults pay $7 for admission, children aged 6 through 11 pay $2, and seniors $6. Tel.: (804) 971–2530.

MONTICELLO STANDS IN CHARLOTTESVILLE, Virginia, as a living monument to Thomas Jefferson, who designed and supervised its construction. When Jefferson began drawing floor plans for Monticello, there were no architects in the American colonies who had built a home such as he envisioned. Architecture was not taught in any American college. To obtain what he wanted, lawyer Jefferson trained himself to be a part-time amateur architect of the highest proficiency. Amassing a rich collection of architectural books, he learned the rules of harmonious proportions. His special mentor was the Venetian architect Palladio. In a handbook by Robert Morris, the British architect, Jefferson found plans for octagonal rooms which showed brick and wood adaptations of Palladio's style. With a valiant disregard for structural difficulties, he selected as models a dome from the temple of Vesta and a Corinthian frieze from a temple of Jupiter, which he set about reproducing, together with some inventions of his own, in a home without precedent in America.

The estate on which Monticello was erected came to Thomas Jefferson from his father, Peter Jefferson, who had received it as a grant in 1735. The idea of building a beautiful home on top of the "little mountain" was first conceived by Jefferson when he was a boy, playing and studying under the trees there. He began drawing the plans for Monticello in 1767, and the work of leveling the site for the building began the following year. Construction, however, did not begin for several years, and because of numerous changes and alterations the three-story house of thirty-five rooms (including twelve in the basement) was not completed until after 1809.

Monticello, at Charlottesville, Virginia, designed by Thomas Jefferson and based on the work of the Venetian architect Palladio. Shown here is the west front. (Photograph by Edwin S. Roseberry.)

In 1769, Jefferson became a member of the Virginia House of Burgesses. Subsequently, he served as a delegate to the Continental Congress (where he was chosen to draft the Declaration of Independence), as governor of Virginia, as minister to France, as Secretary of State under George Washington, as Vice-President of the United States, and then two terms as President of the United States (1801–1809). His later years were devoted to the establishment of the University of Virginia, which he founded in 1819, planning the buildings himself and supervising their construction.

The Monticello plantation site is unique. The artificially created plateau is 857 feet above sea level. To make all parts of the mountain accessible, Jefferson constructed paths or roundabouts on its slopes at four different levels. There is still evidence of these today.

Most of the material for the building was made on the site. The stones for the foundation were quarried from the mountainside, bricks were baked in his own kiln, the timbers cut from his forest, and nails wrought in his own nailery. Even some of the hardware for the mansion was made in his shop, but such things as locks and glass for the doors and windows were purchased.

In those days there was on every plantation a series of small, disconnected out-buildings, such as a laundry, smokehouse, dairy, stables, weaving house and kitchen. With his architectural genius, Jefferson sought to make these as inconspicuous as possible by locating them beneath the long terraces terminating in two balanced out-chambers. Connecting these terraces is the all-weather passageway in which are strategically placed wine room, beer room and ware room.

Aerial view of Monticello (west front) and the entire plantation site.

The east front of Monticello. Weather vane on portico roof can be read from inside the house. (Photograph by Edwin S. Roseberry.)

The first building erected was the small pavilion at the end of the south terrace. It was completed in time for Jefferson to bring there, in January 1772, his bride, Martha Wayles Skelton, a charming widow of twenty-three. The southwest chamber is referred to appropriately enough as the "Honeymoon Cottage." The marriage was a happy one, but short. In ten years Martha died. They had six children—five daughters and one son—only one of whom, Martha, the eldest, survived her father. Another daughter, Mary, grew to womanhood and married but died when she was only twenty-six.

The octagonal Dome Room. (Photograph by Edwin S. Roseberry.)

The mansion itself is one of the classic examples of American architecture. The dominating feature is the dome, which commands the garden, or west front. The octagonal room under the dome is often referred to as the Ball Room, but Jefferson himself called it the Sky, or Dome, Room.

The absence of any important staircase in the main hall is often commented upon. After Jefferson returned from his ministry in France in 1789, he made numerous changes in the plan and design of Monticello. An early floor plan had contained a central stairway to the second floor, but this was now eliminated. Instead, in the interest of economy of space and also probably of privacy, Jefferson constructed two narrow (24-inch), steep and winding staircases, one in each wing, extending from the basement to the third floor.

While abroad, Jefferson had purchased many accessories and ornaments for Monticello—silver, china, candlesticks, linens and works of art—things not readily obtainable in America. Many of these original furnishings are on display on the first floor. Some of Jefferson's innovations, still in use, are the seven-day calendar clock with its cannonball weights, and the double doors between the hall and parlor, which open simultaneously when either is moved. A weather vane on top of the east portico is connected to a dial on the ceiling beneath and can be read from inside the house. Built into the mantel in the dining room are two small dumbwaiters, one on each end, which were used to carry bottles of wine from the cellar. All of the beds are located in alcoves, and in Jefferson's bedroom the alcove also opens into the study. Above this alcove is a closet, reached by a small stairway.

Following Jefferson's retirement to Monticello he had an almost continuous stream of visitors from far and near. Many stayed for days, weeks and even months.

The entrance hall.

Parlor. (Photograph by Edwin S. Roseberry.)

Dining room at Monticello, showing mantel with Wedgwood medallions.

Jefferson's bedroom at Monticello, with revolving table and swivel chair. Staircase (roped off) leads up to a closet over the bed. Jefferson's study can be seen at rear, on the other side of the sleeping alcove. (Courtesy Thomas Jefferson Memorial Foundation.)

Monticello was by far the most interesting and attractive home in America, and Jefferson's engaging personality made these visits enjoyable. But this hospitality was a tremendous drain on the resources of Monticello, and Jefferson's last years were marred by never ending financial worries.

Jefferson died at Monticello at the age of eighty-three on July 4, 1826. He lies buried in the family graveyard, which he laid out on the mountainside adjacent to the road leading from the house to the lodge. Title to this plot has never left the family, which retained it when the estate was sold in 1831. The plot is now maintained by the Monticello Association, an organization of the descendants of Jefferson, whose members have a right of burial there.

Monticello is now owned by the Thomas Jefferson Memorial Foundation, a nonprofit organization founded in 1923. It purchased the property, which now consists of 1,800 acres. The purpose of the foundation is to preserve the house and restore the garden. The gardens on the east and west lawns of Monticello, neglected for many years, were restored in 1939 and 1940 according to Jefferson's original plans. Several drawings were found among his papers showing the arrangement he projected and this was ultimately accomplished. On one is indicated the long gravel walk with its borders that circumscribe the west lawn, as well as the semicircle of shrubs and trees in front of the house. Another shows the arrangement of the oval and circular beds near the house that Jefferson himself laid out in 1807. The plants for each bed are listed in his garden and farm books and the directions were faithfully followed in the restoration. Near the pavilion that terminates the south terrace is the fish pond that Jefferson kept well stocked with fish caught in nearby streams. Today Jefferson's Monticello is much as it was when he retired to enjoy his last years among his family and flowers.

West front of Monticello, showing gravel walk and flowers. The gardens have been restored according to Jefferson's original plans.

5

James Madison

THE OCTAGON IN WASHINGTON, D.C.

HOW TO GET THERE/WHEN TO VISIT

The Octagon is located at 1799 New York Ave., N.W., at 18th St. in Washington, D.C. It is open weekdays except Monday from 10 A.M. to 4 P.M. and weekends from 12 noon to 4 P.M. It is closed Thanksgiving Day, Christmas Day and New Year's Day. There is no fixed admission fee, but a donation is requested. Tel.: (202) 638–3105.

WHEN THE WHITE HOUSE was burned by the British during the War of 1812, President and Mrs. James Madison (Dolley) were forced to live elsewhere while it was being rebuilt. They accepted the hospitality of Colonel John Tayloe, a wealthy Virginia planter, who offered them his unique 18th-century Federal townhouse known as The Octagon.

Colonel Tayloe had originally planned to build a townhouse in Philadelphia, but his close friend President George Washington persuaded him to build it in the new capital city. In 1797, Tayloe purchased a lot and obtained the services of Dr. William Thornton, architect of the Capitol. Built between 1798 and 1800, the house was considered one of the finest in the nation, and in it Colonel Tayloe entertained many distinguished guests including Madison, Thomas Jefferson, James Monroe, John Adams, Andrew Jackson, Stephen Decatur, Daniel Webster, Henry Clay, the Marquis de Lafayette and John Calhoun. In 1814, after the destruction of the White House, the Capitol and other buildings, Colonel Tayloe was among many Washington residents who offered their homes to the President and Mrs. Madison during the rebuilding of the executive mansion. The Madisons first chose The Octagon, living there for nearly a year in 1814 and 1815. They had their bedrooms on the east side of the second floor. President Madison used the round room above the house's entrance as a study, where, on February 17, 1815, he confirmed the Treaty of Ghent, which had ended the War of 1812. In 1815 the Madisons moved to one of the "Seven Buildings" (a series of attached townhouses built in 1796) on Pennsylvania Avenue, living there for the remainder of the President's term of office.

The Octagon in Washington, D.C., home of President and Mrs. James Madison in 1814 and 1815, after the White House had been destroyed by the British. The Madisons occupied a suite of rooms on the second floor. (Photograph by William Edmund Barrett.)

After Mrs. Tayloe's death in 1855, the Tayloe family no longer lived in the house, and it soon fell into disrepair. In 1865 the St. Rose's Technical Institute, a Catholic school for girls, occupied the house, and from 1866 to 1879 the government rented it for the use of the Hydrographic Office. Until about 1885, when the Tayloe heirs entrusted it to a caretaker, it was used as an office and a studio-dwelling. As early as 1889 the American Institute of Architects expressed interest in acquiring the building for its national headquarters; they took possession in 1898, and in 1902 purchased it.

The Treaty Room, where President Madison confirmed the Treaty of Ghent. (Photograph by William Edmund Barrett.)

The Octagon is a three-story red-brick building, trimmed with Aquia sandstone. It is now in the process of a complete restoration. Stone steps lead to a circular entrance area that opens into a foyer. From the foyer a spiral staircase curves upward to the Treaty Room. It has been restored and includes, among other things, the table on which Madison confirmed the Treaty of Ghent. Other second-floor rooms, including the ones used by the Madisons for living quarters, are now exhibition galleries. The garden was restored in 1950 and the A.I.A. has built a new headquarters behind The Octagon.

6

Andrew Jackson

The Hermitage, near Nashville, Tennessee.

HOW TO GET THERE/WHEN TO VISIT

The Hermitage (4580 Rachel's Lane, Hermitage, Tennessee 37076) is 12 miles east of downtown Nashville, off Highway 45 (Old Hickory Blvd.). It can be reached by Interstate 40 east out of Nashville (Exit 221), Interstate 65 north (Exit 92) or Interstate 24 north (Exit 40). Open daily from 9 A.M. to 5 P.M. except for Thanksgiving, Christmas Day and the third week of January. Admission fee (special rates available; call or write for information). Tel.: (615) 889–2941.

ANDREW JACKSON ("OLD HICKORY"), the son of Scots-Irish immigrants, was one of America's most beloved Presidents and one of our great military heroes. His expedition against the Creek Indians in 1813 broke their power in Georgia and Alabama. Two years later, now a major-general in the regular army, he achieved the decisive victory over the British at New Orleans that secured his place in American military history.

As seventh President of the United States, Andrew Jackson impressed himself so powerfully on the times that historians call his administration and the years immediately following "the Age of Jackson." During his presidency the national debt was retired, the federal surplus was returned to the states, and American claims against France were collected.

The years before Jackson's Presidential election were shared with his wife, Rachel, to whom his devotion was great. From 1819 to 1821 he built the Hermitage mansion for her. For fifteen years before the mansion was completed the Jacksons lived in a log-cabin complex near the place where the new house was eventually built. Rachel picked the site, a level meadow, for the house. The bricks with which the house was built were made on the premises. The original Hermitage mansion was a square, two-story house, with four rooms and a large hall downstairs, and a similar arrangement upstairs. In later years, when the mansion was enlarged, the original house remained as the central core.

In December of 1828, Rachel died at the age of sixty-one. Three weeks later, Jackson, elected President just a month earlier, went to Washington. In 1830, two

The Hermitage mansion, Andrew Jackson's home near Nashville, Tennessee, as rebuilt, 1835–37, after a fire had destroyed much of the original 1819–21 house. Jackson had built the house for his wife, Rachel, to whom he was intensely devoted. (Courtesy Ladies' Hermitage Association.)

wings, including a dining room and a library, were added to the Hermitage mansion. Soon afterward, Jackson's adopted son, Andrew Jackson, Jr., and his wife Sarah occupied the mansion.

In 1834 disaster struck. A spark from the back parlor chimney fell on the oak shingle roof and set the house on fire. All that remained were the brick walls and the dining room. Jackson, in Washington serving his second term as President, told his daughter-in-law not to mourn the loss: he would have the mansion rebuilt.

This he did, and the mansion as it appears today was the result. Finished in 1837, it is a much more elaborate structure than the original 1821 house. The builders used the original foundation and the brick walls, but added a façade on the front and two-story porticoes on the front and back. The six tall white columns were also added at that time. This is the stately mansion—with its modified Corinthian columns, wide verandas, spacious front hall and graceful spiral staircase—to which Andrew Jackson returned in 1837 to spend the last eight years of his life receiving visitors from all across the land. He died there on June 5, 1845, at the age of seventy-eight. At his request he was buried beside his beloved Rachel in the tomb that he had ordered built for her in 1831, on the Hermitage grounds, in the back of the garden.

The Hermitage stands on 625 acres of farmland, based on the 425 acres originally purchased by Jackson in 1804. The mansion itself is an interesting example of pre-Civil War Southern Greek Revival architecture. The furnishings, which belonged to the Jackson family—paintings, crystal, mirrors, the huge dining-room table and Jackson's bed—are all there, much as they were when Jackson lived. On display in the museum are countless personal items and gifts from around the world—jewelry, swords, pistols, miniatures, military insignia and copies of Jackson's letters and documents.

The entrance-hall wallpaper was printed by du Four in Paris and the twenty-five strips represent the landing of Telemachus on the island of Calypso during his travels in search of his father, Ulysses. The wallpaper was ordered by Jackson in 1835. The mahogany sofas, pier tables and lovely chandeliers are all matched pieces.

The front parlor is furnished with an Italian marble mantel, a gilded overmantel mirror and a Japanese clock inlaid with enamel.

The back parlor has two special pieces: a mahogany center table, the only piece remaining of the set presented to General and Mrs. Jackson when they visited New Orleans after the battle there that made him a national hero; and a clock, one of the few relics at the Hermitage that were there while Mrs. Jackson was still alive.

Jackson's ground-floor bedroom is much as it was the day he died in its canopy bed. Personal items include his tobacco box, leather hat box, hair and clothes brushes and a French china teapot with a place for a candle at the bottom.

The room that best represents the interests of Jackson is his office or library. For many years it was the political center of the United States and the center of Democratic party affairs.

The dining room on the first (ground) floor is the most historically significant

Hermitage dining room, the only room left intact after the original house burned in 1834. (Courtesy Ladies' Hermitage Association.)

The front parlor. (Courtesy Ladies'
Hermitage Association.)

*Jackson's bedroom at the Her-
mitage, containing the actual bed
used by the General.* (Courtesy
Ladies' Hermitage Association.)

room in the mansion. A number of Presidents, including James Polk and Franklin Delano Roosevelt, have visited it as a historic shrine; Lyndon Baines Johnson was the last President to eat there.

The original Hermitage is represented by the remaining three log cabins (there may have been more or fewer when the farm was purchased), two of which, considerably improved, were occupied by General Jackson and his family during the time he defeated the Creek Indians and became the hero of the battle of New Orleans.

Original log cabin, one of three remaining, on the Hermitage property. The Jacksons lived in such cabins from 1804 to 1821, when the mansion was finished. During this period Jackson became famous as a military man.

"Rachel's Church" or the Hermitage Church was erected in 1823 on land donated by Jackson and at the urging of his wife, Rachel.
(Courtesy Ladies' Hermitage Association.)

Also on view is the Hermitage Church adjacent to Tulip Grove. A historic landmark, it is sometimes called "Rachel's Church." It was erected at Rachel's urging in 1823 on a three-acre plot of land donated to the community by General Jackson. The tomb, in a picturesque corner of the garden, is shaded by hickory trees planted in the 1920s. The garden, designed for Rachel in 1819, is an outstanding example of Early American landscape art. It covers more than an acre and contains dozens of varieties of plants along with beautiful magnolias. Eventually it will be returned to its original function of flower-and-kitchen garden.

7

Martin Van Buren

LINDENWALD, HIS HOME NEAR KINDERHOOK, NEW YORK.

HOW TO GET THERE/WHEN TO VISIT

Lindenwald, between the villages of Kinderhook and Stuyvesant Falls on
the east bank of the Hudson River in upstate New York, is 18 miles south of
Albany on U.S. 9H. It is open from 9 A.M. to 5 P.M. daily from the last week of
April through October 31, and Wednesdays through Sundays from
November 1 through December 5. Admission for persons aged 17 through
61, $1.00; others free. Tel.: (518) 758-9689.

DURING THE FIRST HALF of the 19th century there were few years when Martin Van
Buren was neither a political officeholder nor a candidate. His public career
touched every branch of government, and the respect of his colleagues, including
opponents, for his mastery of political maneuvers is revealed in his many
nicknames: "Little Magician," "Red Fox" and "the American Talleyrand."

Martin Van Buren, the first President born under the American flag, was born in
Kinderhook, New York, on December 5, 1782. His family had come to America from
Amsterdam. His father was a tavern keeper and farmer. Martin left school at
fourteen to become an apprentice lawyer; he was admitted to the bar at twenty and
maintained an active, successful practice which made him financially independent
and led to his entrance into politics.

Van Buren found his milieu in the rough politics of New York State. Beginning
with the office of surrogate and going on to become state senator and attorney
general, Van Buren gained control of a statewide political organization called the
Albany Regency. He used it to establish a political base, winning a seat in the U.S.
Senate in 1821. By 1827, Van Buren had emerged as the principal northern leader for
Andrew Jackson. He served briefly as governor of New York, leaving the position
when President Jackson appointed him Secretary of State as a reward for his
support. But when a conflict developed in the Cabinet between Jackson men and
supporters of Vice-President Calhoun, Van Buren—always politically shrewd—
resigned. This maneuver kept the conflict in check, and the President rewarded Van
Buren with an appointment as ambassador to England. In London, however, he

Lindenwald, home of Martin Van Buren near Kinderhook, New York. The southern Colonial portico was erected in this century by recent owners, replacing Van Buren's heavy Victorian entrance porch. (Photograph by Fred Van Tassell.)

received word that his appointment had not been confirmed by the Senate—the work of Calhoun, who broke a tie by voting against the appointment. Van Buren thus became the martyr of the Jacksonian Democrats, and in 1832 he became Vice-President under Jackson. Jackson's choice of Van Buren as his successor assured the pinnacle of political success for him in 1836.

The campaign of 1836 was the first one in which Presidential candidates traveled about to make speeches and distribute campaign biographies. The rough-and-tumble politics that Van Buren had mastered were now part of the highest office in America. He was elected in 1837.

In 1839 Van Buren purchased Lindenwald, the mansion once owned by a boyhood friend, William Van Ness. He hoped to serve two terms as President before retiring to Lindenwald, but he found himself perhaps the first President to be burdened with the policies of his predecessor, the most disastrous result of which was the Panic of 1837. The boom-and-bust cycle of 19th-century commerce, abetted by Jackson's fiscal policy, fell upon Van Buren, and while he had not caused the depression, he was a handy scapegoat, especially so because he had a penchant for elegance and rich living. Thus, in 1840, in the "Log Cabin and Hard Cider" campaign of William Henry Harrison, a Virginia aristocrat who posed as one of the "common people," Van Buren, one of the most truly democratic Presidents, became associated with gold spoons and revelry and was defeated by a log-cabin myth.

He lost his party's nomination in 1844 because of his opposition to the annexation of Texas and the attendant threat of war. His growing inclination against the expansion of slavery led to his final candidacy for President on the Free Soil Ticket in 1848, although he maintained his interest in politics until his death in 1862.

Lindenwald was built in 1797 by Peter Van Ness. The builder's son, William, inherited the property upon his father's death in 1804 and retained it until 1824. During this period Washington Irving was a frequent guest and for a time was tutor to the Van Ness children. William Paulding, Jr., bought the house at an auction in 1824, and in 1839 Van Buren bought the property, which consisted of the house and 130 acres. In the next six years he purchased additional land, bringing his holdings to 220 acres. While living at Lindenwald, the former President, a widower, enjoyed the families of his sons as well as a number of famous visitors including Henry Clay, Sam Tilden and Winfield Scott.

Since Van Buren's death the property has changed hands several times. One owner, Leonard Jerome, was the maternal grandfather of Winston Churchill. The present property, consisting of 12.8 acres, was purchased by Mr. and Mrs. Kenneth Campbell in 1957.

Lindenwald represents a series of alterations and additions extending from its construction in the late 18th century into the 20th century. The original house is a substantial Federal type with finely executed interior woodwork, mantels and trim; plaster cornices; fluted baseboards; Palladian entrance door; and a central Palladian window above the entrance. What was probably the first major alteration occurred in 1841 with the removal of the stairway in the first floor central hall to create a Palladian-style banquet hall or ballroom approximately 42 feet long by 15 feet wide. The stair was relocated to an enclosure in the den, with the resulting alcove, formed off the south parlor, in the Gothic style in contrast to the classic Federal woodwork of the room. The banquet hall, possibly the first of the Van Buren alterations, still retains its original features, including the French wallpaper *Paysage à Chasses.*

In 1849, Van Buren engaged Richard Upjohn to design a wing which was added to the rear and formed an ell on the southwest. This addition, with its brick tower, was in the Italianate style. Also a part of the Van Buren additions was a heavily styled Victorian entrance porch. Two dormers and a central gable were added to the

North side of Lindenwald, in original Federal style. (Photograph by Fred Van Tassell.)

South side of Lindenwald, showing Italianate wing and tower added in 1849. (Photograph by Fred Van Tassell.)

front roof slope of the 1797 portion and a dormer on the rear slope to light the third floor. Two original windows in each of the end gables were closed at that time.

The 1797 house and the 1849 addition comprise a total of thirty-six rooms and passageways. Most of the rooms are located at the basement and first-floor levels. The 20th-century additions by recent owners include a southern Colonial portico extending across the front, which replaced the Van Buren Victorian entrance; a screened porch; and fenestration alterations on the southeast corner. These were all removed after the National Park Service took over the estate in 1976.

Another view of the tower and wing, from the rear, or southwest side, of the house. (Photograph by Fred Van Tassell.)

44

Entrance hall, left of front door. Pictures at right show the house as it was in earlier periods. (Photograph by Fred Van Tassell.)

Lindenwald interior: archway between Red Room and den, on the first floor off the large ballroom. (Photograph by Fred Van Tassell.)

Martin Van Buren 45

The main portion of the Van Buren house is brick, two and a half stories tall on a stone basement foundation. The Upjohn addition is a large one-story wing of brick with sandstone trim on brick basement walls. The Italianate tower is approximately four stories high with the top level open on two sides to form an observation platform and bell tower. The sides of the tower are pierced with round-headed lancet windows to light the tower stairs; they match the Romanesque windows in the addition. The windows are repeated in larger scale on the enclosed ends of the tower. The exterior brick walls were painted cream and the trim red during the historic period.

Mirror in the Red Room. (Photograph by Fred Van Tassell.)

Mantel in the banquet hall. Van Buren hoped to leave office a revered elder statesman and expected to entertain many guests in the large banquet hall built out of the original house's central hallway. But he left the Presidency in disfavor, owing largely to the depression that marked his administration. The banquet hall was seldom used. (Photograph by Fred Van Tassell.)

The mansion has remained relatively unchanged since the historic period. Most of the original hardware remains, including silver-plated knobs and hardware on the first floor and carpenter locks on the second floor. The greatest changes were due to the installation of modern kitchens and bathrooms. The original kitchen and service quarters were located in the basement, and the early kitchen range, with ovens installed by Van Buren, is intact. Modern kitchens, installed by later owners in former bedrooms on the first and second floors, have been removed by the National Park Service in the interest of historic authenticity.

Additional points of interest are an unusually large lobby on the second floor, the two first-floor indoor necessaries added by Van Buren, and the 1848 furnace in the basement. There are two gatehouses, erected by Van Buren at the two entrances to the estate on the Albany Post Road.

The Lindenwald estate, now on the Martin Van Buren National Historic Site, was fully restored by the National Park Service in 1987 to its appearance in Van Buren's era.

8

William Henry Harrison

BERKELEY, HIS BIRTHPLACE NEAR CHARLES CITY, VIRGINIA;
AND GROUSELAND, HIS HOME IN VINCENNES, INDIANA.

HOW TO GET THERE/WHEN TO VISIT

Berkeley is located about eight miles west of Charles City, on Route 5
between Williamsburg and Richmond, Virginia. It is open daily from 8 A.M.
to 5 P.M. Closed Christmas Day. Adult admission, $7.00; students (13–18),
$4.00; children 6–12, $3.00; children under 6, free. Tel.: (804) 795-2453.

Grouseland is located at 3 West Scott Street, off Harrison Street near the
Indiana Territorial Capitol Building in Vincennes, Indiana. It is open
daily from 9 A.M. to 5 P.M. (11 A.M. to 4 P.M. in January and February) except
Thanksgiving, Christmas and New Year's days. Admission, $2.00, except
children under 12, 50 cents. For information write to "Grouseland," 3 West
Scott Street, Vincennes, IN 47591.

THE FIRST RUMBLES OF the Revolutionary War were being heard when William
Henry Harrison was born on February 9, 1773, at Berkeley, his grandfather's estate
at Charles City on the James River in Virginia. His father, the fifth Benjamin
Harrison, was a signer of the Declaration of Independence and three times governor
of Virginia.

William Henry inherited 3,000 acres when his father died, but no money to pay
off any debts. The necessity to earn money forced him to leave the medical school of
the University of Pennsylvania and accept a commission as ensign in the First U.S.
Regiment of Infantry. At that time the regular army consisted of this single infantry
regiment and an artillery battalion. In time he was promoted to captain, and while
he was at Fort Washington he met and eloped with Anna Symmes, daughter of John
Cleves Symmes, owner of vast tracts of Ohio land.

He left the army to become Secretary of the Northwest Territory at a salary of
$1,200 a year. In 1799 he was elected to Congress and in 1800 was appointed the first
governor of Indiana Territory by President Adams. Indiana Territory was established on July 4 of that year, comprising the present states of Indiana, Illinois,

Berkeley, the birthplace of William Henry Harrison and the ancestral home of Benjamin Harrison, his grandson, near Charles City, Virginia. (Photograph by Taylor Lewis & Associates.)

Michigan, Wisconsin and parts of Minnesota. Vincennes was named the capital of the territory.

As governor one of his duties was to amass land for his government. In 1809, by the Treaty of Fort Wayne, he secured two and one-half million acres of Indiana territory. Tecumseh, a Shawnee chief, denounced the treaty and organized opposition among various Indian tribes. On November 6–8, 1811, Harrison led a military expedition at Tippecanoe Creek and won a major battle in the wars against the Indians. He became commander-in-chief of the Army of the Northwest in 1812, reoccupied Detroit, and won an impressive victory at the Battle of the Thames in Canada in 1813.

After the War of 1812 Harrison reentered politics and was elected to the U.S. Senate. In 1840 he was elected President as the "log cabin" Whig candidate. It was ironic that this aristocratic Virginia gentleman was elected because of his public image as a "spit and swear" feisty general. He died of pneumonia after serving only thirty-one days. He was buried at North Bend, Ohio.

Berkeley has a distinction shared only with the Adams house in Massachusetts: it was the ancestral home of two Presidents—the birthplace of William Henry Harrison, our ninth President, and the ancestral home of his grandson, Benjamin Harrison, our twenty-third President.

Berkeley is a beautiful, excellently restored example of the brick mansions that graced Virginia's "Golden Age." Built in 1726 by the fourth Benjamin Harrison, grandfather of William Henry, it is believed to be the oldest three-story brick house in Virginia.

It was built on a rise about one-quarter mile back from the river, with a lovely vista of hills and water. Its walls are three feet thick, its floors are of handhewn heart-pine, and it has one of the first pediment roofs in Virginia. There are three dormers on each of the fronts.

The main house is flanked by two smaller, two-story buildings. To the east is the Bachelor's House, where William Henry and his brothers and sisters attended school. To the west is the kitchen and servants' quarters, connected to the main house by a brick passageway.

The twelve-foot-wide central hall is divided in the middle by an arch supported by fluted pilasters. Very little of the original trim and paneling remains; about 1790, Benjamin Harrison had new paneling installed in place of the original. The interior finish from the early period is exemplified by the mottled-gray marble facing of the back-to-back fireplaces on the east chimney. These fireplaces open on the north and south parts of the Great Room and are connected on each side of the chimney by an arched alcove. There is a little musician's balcony on the second landing.

The dining room is perhaps the showpiece. A portrait of Benjamin Harrison IV hangs over the mantel. Artifacts include blue and white Chinese porcelain, old English silver, a Waterford glass chandelier from Ireland, a set of Hepplewhite chairs, a three-section dining table and an eighteenth-century walnut corner cupboard from Virginia. One of the finest pieces in the room is a gentleman's chest, *circa* 1725, of curly cherry wood. The hall contains a Chippendale cherry linen press.

Berkeley did not escape unscathed in American wars. In 1781 it was plundered by British troops under Benedict Arnold. During the Civil War it served as headquarters for General McClellan after his withdrawal from the Battle of Malvern Hill. More than 100,000 Federal troops were encamped in its fields, and transports and gunboats were anchored in the James. While quartered nearby in the summer of 1862, General Butterfield composed "Taps." At this time the estate was known as "Harrison's Landing."

William Henry Harrison returned to Berkeley to write his inaugural address in the room in which he had been born.

The north (top photo) and south (right) parts of the Great Room, Berkeley. Back-to-back fireplaces open on each part and are connected on each side of the chimney by an arched alcove. Period furniture comes from "Westover," an adjoining plantation. (Photographs by Walter H. Miller.)

Dining room at Berkeley. A portrait of Benjamin Harrison, grandfather of William Henry, looks out on old English silver, Hepplewhite chairs, Waterford glass and Chinese porcelain. (Photograph by Walter H. Miller.)

Grouseland, the home of William Henry Harrison in Vincennes, Indiana, then the capital of the new Indiana Territory. Harrison, newly appointed governor of the territory, brought with him to the frontier town the traditions of Virginia living and thus built his new house on a grand scale that would help him maintain this tradition and enhance his prestige as governor. Shown here is the River Side, or Bow End.

Harrison was just thirty, with most of his career ahead of him, when he started to build Grouseland in 1803. It was originally built as two buildings, the larger "great house" in front and the "dependency" to the rear.

A covered passage joined the two buildings, forming between them a service hall in the main floor and a narrow servants' corridor on the second floor. This addition may have been Harrison's way of dealing with the severe Indiana winters, to which a Virginian would not be accustomed.

The first floor of the great house includes the bow-end Council Chamber, which was used for meetings and entertainment, and the family dining room.

The Council Chamber contains hand-carved mantels, English window glass, chair rails of black walnut, and sashes and doors made by craftsmen in Chillicothe and Pittsburgh. There is a portrait of young Harrison by Rembrandt Peale. The glazed yellow wallpaper is bordered with blue swags. The Martha Washington chairs are upholstered in yellow. The most treasured piece in the room is Harrison's cherry pedestal table.

The dining room is papered in the tradition of the best homes of the day and has an original family sideboard. It contains a portrait of Jane Findlay Harrison, wife of William Henry Harrison II, who served as her father-in-law's hostess in the White House.

A graceful "Virginia" stairway with cherry treads and banisters leads to the second-floor hall, which functions as a room, offering sleeping space for guests.

Another view of Grouseland. The heavy shutters were a precaution against Indian attacks.

Harrison dining room. The sideboard (right rear), given to Mrs. Harrison by her father, set the pattern for the furnishings of this room when it was restored.

The yellow and white wallpaper with a classical arch motif is carried from the lower hall and staircase. Much of the furniture was made in early-19th-century Indiana, with strong, simple lines. Fine examples can be seen in the southeast bedroom, believed to be Harrison's. The Federal-style fireplace was carved in Vincennes. The small Windsor chair, table and blanket chest belonged to the Harrisons.

The building has many fortress-like details designed to guard the house against Indian attacks. The eighteen-inch outer walls are slit to make portholes; the attic windows are designed for sharpshooters, and the six-foot-high windows are fitted with heavy shutters inside and out. There is a powder magazine in the cellar with heavy masonry walls, and a trapdoor through an arched ceiling of brick leads to a rooftop lookout.

Entrance hall, with "Virginia" stairway. The cherry treads are set far back into the wall so that the stairway is self-supporting.

The west bedroom, with the sturdy, simply designed furniture made in early-19th-century Indiana. The Harrisons had many guests. As governor, William often invited legislators to live at Grouseland while attending sessions, and during Indian scares, townspeople were invited to "move in" to the well-protected house.

Harrison, his wife and eight children remained in Grouseland until 1812. At that time Judge Benjamin Parke occupied the house for a period. In 1819 John Cleves Symmes Harrison, the eldest son, was appointed receiver of the land office in Vincennes, and in 1821 the house was deeded to him. He lived there for about ten years. Grouseland was held by the family until 1850.

For a time it was used as a storage for grain. When the railroad came, it was a hotel. It became a private residence again from 1860 to 1909. It was opened as a historic house museum in 1911 by the Francis Vigo Chapter of the D.A.R., which has maintained it to this day.

9

John Tyler

SHERWOOD FOREST, THE HOME IN CHARLES CITY COUNTY, VIRGINIA.

HOW TO GET THERE/WHEN TO VISIT

The **Sherwood Forest** plantation is located 30 miles east of Richmond and 20 miles west of Williamsburg along Route 5, the highway named in Tyler's honor. Harrison Tyler, the present owner, opens the house to the public by appointment for group visits. Grounds open daily from 9 A.M. to 5 P.M. Tel.: (804) 829–5377.

JOHN TYLER WAS THE first Vice-President to succeed to the Presidency, assuming the office on the death of William Henry Harrison in 1841. Tyler's political career was distinguished: Virginia state senator and member of the Virginia house of delegates, governor of Virginia, member of the House of Representatives, United States senator, tenth President of the United States from 1841 to 1845, president of the peace commission of 1861 and member of the Confederate Congress.

His estate, originally called Creek Plantation, was named Sherwood Forest by President Tyler, who likened himself to Robin Hood. The original house, built in 1720, was renovated and doubled in size by Tyler after he purchased it in 1842. He connected the old kitchen and laundry to the house on the east end by a covered colonnade and added a corresponding west wing for his office and a ballroom. The latter, with its unique arched ceiling, is one of the rooms open to visitors. Opposite one end of the house is the 18th-century wine house, and opposite the other, the old dairy. All the buildings are in a twenty-five-acre yard with more than eighty varieties of old trees, averaging 200 years old.

The house—300 feet long and one room deep with the central portion three stories—is the longest frame dwelling in America. Begun in 1720, this Colonial-and Empire-period structure, with its clapboard exterior, remains largely as it appeared when Tyler retired from the White House in 1845, making Sherwood Forest his home until his death in 1862.

Occupied continuously by the Tyler family, the Sherwood Forest home contains much of the original furniture and effects of the President. A portrait of him hangs

Sherwood Forest, the home of John Tyler in Charles City County, Virginia. It is 300 feet long, in Colonial and Empire styles, and contains much original family furniture. (Photograph by Walter H. Miller.)

in the hall. The wallpaper in the dining room dates from 1844. Across the hall, facing her husband, hangs a portrait of Mrs. Tyler, the former Julia Gardiner of Long Island. The majority of the furnishings are original, a magnificent collection of 18th- and 19th-century antiques, including silver, oriental rugs and various objets d'art.

10

James Knox Polk

THE BIRTHPLACE SITE AT PINEVILLE, NORTH CAROLINA;
AND THE ANCESTRAL HOME IN COLUMBIA, TENNESSEE.

HOW TO GET THERE/WHEN TO VISIT

The **Polk birthplace site** is on Highway 521 at Pineville, south of Charlotte, North Carolina. From April 1 through October 31 it is open Monday through Saturday from 9 A.M. to 5 P.M. and on Sunday from 1 to 5 P.M. The rest of the year hours are Tuesday through Saturday from 10 A.M. to 4 P.M. and on Sunday from 1 to 5 P.M. Hours may vary; contact site manager (Box 475, Pineville, NC 28134; tel. [704] 889-7145) for details. No admission fee.

The **ancestral home** is at 301 West 7th Street in Columbia, Tennessee, 48 miles south of Nashville at the intersection of highways 43 and 412. Open Monday through Saturday from 9 A.M. to 5 P.M. (November through March to 4 P.M.) and Sunday from 1 to 5 P.M. Closed Thanksgiving, December 24 and 25, January 1. The admission fee is $2.50 for adults, $1 for students (ages 6–18). Tel.: (615) 388-2354.

JAMES K. POLK, ELEVENTH President of the United States—known as the "Napoleon of the Stump"; his original family name was Pollock—was born in Mecklenburg County, North Carolina, on November 2, 1795. When he was eleven, the family moved to a farm in Maury County, Tennessee. After attending nearby academies, he entered the sophomore class of the University of North Carolina in 1815, graduating in 1818 with high honors.

He returned to Tennessee to practice law, and his success as a lawyer brought him into politics. In 1825 he was elected to the first of his seven terms in Congress, and in 1835 he was chosen Speaker of the House. He became governor of Tennessee in 1839, but was defeated in two subsequent races for the post.

On January 1, 1824, he married Sarah Childress of Murfreesboro. Sarah, educated at the Salem Female Academy, a Moravian school in Salem, North Carolina, frequently served as his personal secretary. The Polks had no children.

Polk became the first "dark horse" in American politics when the Democrats chose him over Martin Van Buren as nominee for President against Henry Clay, the Whig choice in 1844. The chief issues of the campaign were the reannexation of Texas and the reoccupation of Oregon, both of which Polk favored. With the battle cry "Fifty-four Forty or Fight," Polk rode into the White House.

Determined, strong and stubborn, he was known as a man of absolute honesty and integrity, and these characteristics marked his administration. He had campaigned with the intention of serving only one term and of accomplishing four major goals.

Two of these were to settle the Oregon question and to acquire California. With the achievement of these objectives, the territory of our nation stretched from the Atlantic to the Pacific for the first time. Other goals included a reduction of the tariff and reestablishment of an independent treasury. And three new states were admitted to the Union: Texas in 1845, Iowa in 1846 and Wisconsin in 1848. During these years the Mormon state of Utah was established and settled.

It was a prosperous time: Gold was discovered in California; the war with Mexico boosted the economy; immigration increased; and numerous machines were invented, of which the sewing machine was the most important.

Polk's most noteworthy accomplishments were obscured by the thunderclouds preceding the Civil War and after that by the long years of Reconstruction. He founded the United States Naval Academy; he forced Britain to conclude a treaty which gave America for the first time her full rights on the high seas; and he acquired New Mexico and California for the United States. To do this he had to fight the unpopular war with Mexico. Three months after his term he died at fifty-four, a martyr to the public service.

A log cabin, believed to be similar to the original Polk birthplace, has been constructed on part of the original Polk family land. It is a story-and-a-half,

Reconstruction of the log-cabin birthplace of James K. Polk at Pineville, North Carolina. (Photo by Larry Misenheimer; courtesy North Carolina Museum of History.)

Kitchen interior (reconstruction) at the Polk birthplace site. Furnishings here and in the main cabin date from the late 1700s to the early 1800s.

two-pen log house measuring 16 by 32 feet with two rooms on each floor and a fireplace on one end. Both the log house and an accompanying kitchen contain furnishings dating from the late 1700s to the early 1800s. Exhibits and films depicting events in Polk's life are shown at the visitors' center of the historic site. Guided tours of the log buildings are given throughout the day.

While young James Polk was away at school in 1816, his father, Samuel, built the ancestral home at Columbia, Tennessee. This is the only house now existing, other than the White House, in which Polk lived.

Modest in size, typical of its locality and period, the Polk home is of handmade brick. The architect is not known. Samuel Polk may have designed and built the house himself.

The Holland method of bricklaying is used on the west side of the building, while the usual type is employed elsewhere. The gutter heads are of special design, and the front door is typically Colonial, with fan-shaped transom.

The furnishings are largely those used by the President and Mrs. Polk in the White House, but there are also items used by Polk in his Columbia law office, some from Polk Place—the Polks' retirement home in Nashville, which was demolished after his death—and some used in the Samuel Polk family.

On the lower floor are the entrance hall, the parlor and the dining room. The hall and three rooms constitute the upper floor. Downstairs the floors are of wide white ash, held together with wooden pegs. Yellow poplar, hand pinned, is used upstairs. Most of the mantels are original. So, too, is the stone hearth in the front parlor. The woodwork, window frames and sash are handmade; there is a slight difference in the height and width of the windows.

The house contains a large collection of outstanding portraits, including the Presidential companion portraits by G. P. A. Healy. Pieces from the four services of

The James K. Polk ancestral home in Columbia, Tennessee. Other than the White House, this Federal-style structure is the only surviving Polk residence. (Courtesy James K. Polk Memorial Association.)

china used in the White House are displayed with the silver, crystal and candelabra used for state dinners.

There are many personal items of the President and Mrs. Polk, including Mrs. Polk's ballgown, designed and made by Worth of Paris. There is the beautiful fan that Polk had made for Mrs. Polk and which she carried to the inaugural ball. The front of the fan has the portraits of the first eleven Presidents, while the back portrays the signing of the Declaration of Independence.

The rosewood and crimson brocade furniture and the mirrors were used in the drawing room at Polk Place. The handmade center table was a gift to the President after his retirement from office. It is a circular slab of black Egyptian marble, inlaid with a mosaic of colored marbles representing the American eagle bearing the coat of arms of the United States and surrounded by thirty white stars standing for the states then composing the Union. The bronze eagle surmounted the entrance gate to Polk Place.

Other buildings that are part of the Polk properties are the kitchen and the museum next door known as the Sisters' House because it was once occupied by the families of the President's sisters. Behind these buildings are gardens patterned after other gardens typical of the period in which the President and his wife lived. This area is entered through the court of the home. True to tradition, it is enclosed by a wall of mellowed handmade brick from one of Maury County's oldest houses, with some of the bricks bearing the date 1807. The garden is formal, with small English boxwoods lining the beds and walks of old moss-covered brick forming the pattern.

The parlor seen from the dining room. These rooms feature rosewood furniture, ormolu chandeliers, an English pianoforte and original White House china. (Courtesy James K. Polk Memorial Association.)

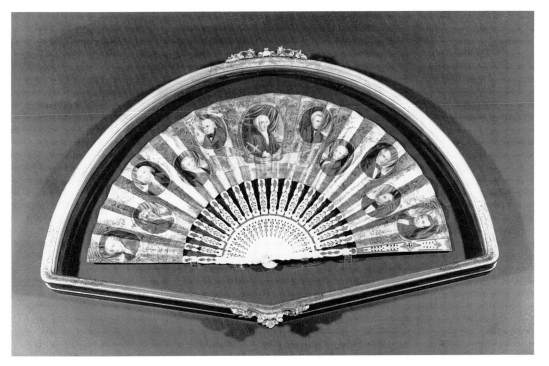

The famous hand-painted fan that President Polk had specially made for Mrs. Polk to carry to his inaugural ball. (Courtesy James K. Polk Memorial Association.)

11

Millard Fillmore

THE BIRTHPLACE REPLICA AT MORAVIA, NEW YORK.

HOW TO GET THERE/WHEN TO VISIT

The Summerhill home replica stands in Fillmore Glen State Park in Moravia, New York. It can be reached by following Interstate 38 to Moravia and watching for appropriate signs directing the visitor to the park, which is one mile south of the center of town. There are no fixed visiting hours and no charge for admission, but a fee is charged for vehicles entering the park. Tel.: (315) 497-0130.

MILLARD FILLMORE, THE THIRTEENTH President of the United States, was born in a log cabin January 7, 1800, a few miles east of Moravia in central New York, the first President and Vice-President born in the 1800s. His father Nathaniel had migrated to New York with his wife Phoebe from Vermont about 1798. The section in which they had settled was wilderness, the nearest neighbor four miles away. Few settlements existed west of Utica, and it would be twenty-five years before the Erie Canal was completed to bring some civilization to this section.

Fillmore's education was meager. He attended the country schools until he was fourteen, when he was bound out as an apprentice to learn the trade of clothmaker at Sparta. At eighteen he abandoned this to study law with Judge Wood of Montville, who loaned Fillmore his *Blackstone's Commentaries.* In 1820 he went to East Aurora, and within three years he was practicing law. In 1830 he moved his practice and his residence to nearby Buffalo.

During this period he attracted the attention of politicians by his delivery of a Fourth of July oration. At twenty-eight he was a member of the New York Assembly, serving for three years. Following this he was a member for eight years of the House of Representatives, where he served on the influential House Ways and Means Committee.

One of his notable achievements as a member of the New York Legislature was a bill eliminating imprisonment for debt, a major reform later adopted by other states.

In 1847 he was elected state comptroller. His support of the enlargement of the

Replica of Millard Fillmore log-cabin birthplace at Moravia, New York.

Erie Canal brought him to such political prominence that it prompted the Whigs in 1848 to nominate him for the Vice-Presidency on a ticket with Zachary Taylor, the Mexican War hero. As Vice-President he presided over the Senate at a time of fierce debates over slavery. When Taylor died in office on July 9, 1850, Fillmore became President.

He was at the helm at a critical time. He did not believe in slavery but he felt even more strongly about holding the states together. He supported the Compromise of 1850 and signed the Fugitive Slave Law even though he knew it would draw upon his head "vials of wrath." He also knew this might cost him his political career—which it did. Because the Fugitive Slave Law was being ignored for the most part in the North, a convention was called in Nashville on November 12, 1850, with talk of secession. As Commander-in-Chief of the armed forces, Fillmore sent troops into North and South Carolina and stopped all threats of insurrection.

Through his influence the Compromise of 1850 became law and undoubtedly postponed the Civil War for eleven years.

Fillmore left the Presidency on March 4, 1853. In 1855 he toured Ireland, England, Italy, France, Prussia, Egypt and Turkey. Queen Victoria pronounced him the most handsome man she had ever seen. In England he refused an honorary D.C.L. degree from Oxford University, stating, "I had not the advantage of a classical education and no man should, in my judgment, accept a degree he cannot read."

His first wife, the former Abigail Powers, whom he had married in 1826, died in 1853. In 1858 he married a forty-five-year-old childless widow, Mrs. Caroline C.

McIntosh. The ceremony took place at Schuyler Mansion, Albany, in the same room in which Alexander Hamilton had married Elizabeth Schuyler seventy-five years earlier. Fillmore died on March 8, 1874.

His two homes in the Moravia area, at Summerhill and New Hope, were torn down. However, there is a replica of the Summerhill home. (His two homes in Buffalo are also gone.)

The Millard Fillmore Birthplace Log Cabin is a replica of the original cabin that could have been built between 1795 and 1797. There are no records to substantiate these dates but local historians base them upon style of construction, history of the site, etc. According to contemporary newspaper accounts, the original cabin was torn down in 1852.

The replica was based on a standard style current for the period. It was done in what historians call "Swedish" construction, similar to the log cabins built by Swedes in Maryland after their arrival in 1632. The cabin is furnished with artifacts from the period 1800-30, and these furnishings have been contributed by local residents.

The replica measures 21 feet by 16 feet, with a single floor and a loft. There are three windows and two doors. The chinking was done with mortar mixed with animal and human hair, similar to the chinking done in early cabins. The five roof rafters were joined at the peak by wooden pegs braced with vertical logs and shingled with cedar shakes. Floor boards were used from old local structures and all of the ironwork, namely hinges, latch, locks and fireplace crane, were handforged by the blacksmith at Colonial Williamsburg. The cabin was dedicated in 1965.

12

Franklin Pierce

THE HOUSE IN CONCORD, NEW HAMPSHIRE.

HOW TO GET THERE/WHEN TO VISIT

The **Franklin Pierce house** at 52 South Main Street, Concord, N.H., can be visited by appointment: write to Curator, Franklin Pierce House, 52 South Main St., Concord, NH 03301. There are no admission charges. Closed from Christmas to April 1.

In 1852, FRANKLIN PIERCE was elected our fourteenth President, carrying all but four states. He served at a time when the United States was becoming increasingly divided by the slavery issue. Pierce felt strongly that the question could be settled without bloodshed, as England and the South American countries had done. Thus, he antagonized many of his New England supporters when he backed the states' rights views of the South. Perhaps his sympathy for the South stemmed from his experience in the Mexican War, where he became acquainted with then-Captain Robert E. Lee and Captain Jefferson Davis of the Mississippi Rifles.

On the other hand, President Pierce had many Northern and abolitionist friends. In fact, he is said to have been acquainted with more nationally famous personages than any other man of his day. He attended Bowdoin College with Nathaniel Hawthorne and Henry Wadsworth Longfellow. He was a loyal supporter of President Jackson, whom he visited at the Hermitage. During his duties in the Senate he knew Henry Clay, John Calhoun, James Buchanan, Daniel Webster and John Quincy Adams. Although a political opponent of Daniel Webster's, he was on the friendliest terms with him and was a frequent visitor at Webster's home. The Fifty-Second Congress Encyclopedia Index states, "But for the opening of the slavery question, Pierce's administration would have been one of the most credible in the nation's history," and, "Of all American executives, Franklin Pierce is preeminently entitled to the designation of the Constitutional President. The great covenant of American liberty was the guide whose precepts he followed without deviation, and posterity will eventually delight to honor him for his wisdom, fairness, and unpartiality."

When his term expired in 1857, President and Mrs. Pierce returned to private life

The bedroom in which Pierce died on October 8, 1869.

and the house at 52 South Main Street in Concord. This was the Pierces' home for the rest of their lives.

Willard Williams, a close friend of the Pierces' and foreman at the Abbot Downing Coach Company, built the house while Pierce was in office. Designed in the French style popular in the pre–Civil War years, the three-story mansard-roof house was on a site well above street level. A wrought-iron fence with stone posts and wide stone steps leading up to the double doors gave the house the air of being quite a suitable residence for a former President. The rooms at the time of his occupancy were a parlor, wide hall, sitting room and dining room on the first floor and five rooms on the second floor. In the rear of the building were a large kitchen and spacious pantries.

Years after President Pierce's death in 1869, the house was used for a time as a church. The beautiful circular stairway and a forty-foot span of wall were removed by a Swedish Baptist congregation, which held services in the long parlor.

After the Baptists had vacated the house, it stood for years as a deteriorating empty shell until John Gravelle, a retired railroader, bought it and set out to restore it. He put back the partition and a similar, though not identical, staircase. He and his wife scoured shops and sought out people who had bought the Pierces' furniture. As a result, Pierce's bedroom looks much as it did when the President slept there. His own bedroom set, hanging kerosene lamp, and portraits on the wall are as they might have been in 1865. The Chickering piano is the original one. A second bedroom, which often sheltered Nathaniel Hawthorne, a lifelong Pierce family friend, is restored. The period decor includes ornate mirrors, an elegantly carved matched settee, chairs covered in purple velvet, lighting fixtures, pictures, flowers, stuffed birds under a glass dome and Currier portraits of the Presidents.

The Gravelles subsidize the support of the Pierce house by catering banquets, wedding parties, etc., in an atmosphere of candlelight, old china and crystal. They have acquired the art of cooking with huge iron and wooden utensils in the old-fashioned kitchen.

13

James Buchanan

WHEATLAND IN LANCASTER, PENNSYLVANIA.

HOW TO GET THERE/WHEN TO VISIT

Wheatland is located at 1120 Marietta Avenue (Rte. 23) in Lancaster, Pennsylvania. It is open for tours daily (except Thanksgiving) from 10 A.M. to 4:15 P.M., April 1 through November 30. Special Christmas Candlelight Tours also given in early December (telephone for details). Admission for adults is $4.00; special rates for seniors, children and students. Group rates (10 or more people) by appointment only. Tel.: (717) 392-8721.

JAMES BUCHANAN, PRESIDENT OF the United States from 1857 to 1861, and with many years of experience as a legislator and diplomat, typified the man of dignity and gracious hospitality of the early 19th century.

Wheatland was built in 1828 for William Jenkins, a Lancaster lawyer who named the estate "The Wheatlands" because of the fields of waving grain surrounding the house. Buchanan acquired it in 1848 from William Meredith, a Philadelphia jurist who had purchased it as a summer residence. He sold the house and its 22 acres to Buchanan, who was then Secretary of State, for the same price he paid for it: $6,750.

There Buchanan led the life of a country gentleman. Wheatland was to be his home for the rest of his life, with two interruptions—his assignment to England as minister to the Court of St. James in 1853 and his departure for the White House as President in 1857.

With Buchanan suggested as a Presidential candidate of the Democratic party on a number of occasions, Wheatland became the scene of many political discussions in the pre–Civil War years. At Wheatland in June 1856, Buchanan first received the news that he had been nominated for the Presidency. Students from Franklin and Marshall College, where he was President of the Board of Trustees, raced from the telegraph office to bring him the news. He departed for his inauguration in March 1857, his carriage escorted by bands and cheering people, to take a special train, its windows decorated with scenes of Wheatland. Four years later, he returned to the front porch of Wheatland, welcomed by cannon salutes and ringing bells, for the peace and quiet of private life.

Wheatland, James Buchanan's home in Lancaster, Pennsylvania. Except when he was minister to England (1853–56) and President (1857–61), Buchanan, a bachelor, lived here with his niece, a housekeeper and a few servants from 1849 until his death in 1868.

70

Buchanan's library and study at Wheatland containing his law books and much of his original furniture. Windows have the original venetian blinds with carved cornices.

The dining room, with the table set for the fruit-and-wine course of a formal dinner. (Courtesy The James Buchanan Foundation for the Preservation of Wheatland.)

There, during the years of the Civil War, the bachelor ex-President lived with his small household—his niece, Miss Harriet Lane, his housekeeper, Miss Hetty Parker, and a few servants. His nephew, James Buchanan Henry, who was now married and practicing law in New York City, visited as frequently as possible.

Today, Wheatland remains much as it was during President Buchanan's day. Its architecture is Federal. The central portion of the building is square. On either side are three-story wings set back from the middle structure. The front porch, from which the President often greeted or said good-bye to guests, has steps on three sides, and the arched doorway is framed by four white pillars.

Buchanan's library and study is one of the most historically important rooms in the house. Buchanan met with political callers and also composed his inaugural address there. Much of his original furniture is on view there today.

In the formal dining room, the great dining table, used by the Buchanan household, is now kept set for the wine-and-fruit course of a gentleman's dinner. The parlor, to the left of the entrance hall, is furnished in early Victorian style. Social gatherings and informal musicales took place there. The Chickering piano that belonged to Harriet Lane remains in fine condition, and some of her music is still in place. There is a fine marble fireplace beneath a great mirror that reflects the light of the gasolier. Delicately carved chairs and marbletop tables add to the atmosphere. The room contains signed portraits of Queen Victoria and her consort, Prince Albert, who came to know Buchanan well when he was minister to England (1853–56). A portrait of the Prince of Wales commemorates his visit in 1860, when he was entertained at the White House by Buchanan and Harriet Lane.

The original venetian blinds, still in place, include elaborately carved wooden cornices equipped with wooden pulleys and cord locks with the original handmade French tapestry tapes. (Venetian blinds are one of the oldest types of window shades, introduced into Venice after Marco Polo's trip to the Far East. Both Thomas Jefferson and George Washington had them installed in their homes.)

A graceful stairway, with mahogany banister and curly maple spindles, leads to the upper hallway from the rear hall. The stairway features an interesting relic of historic folklore in the "Peace Stone," a small glass medallion set into the top of the

Emperor's Bowl, a gift of the Japanese to President Buchanan upon the opening of diplomatic relations with Japan in 1860.

The parlor, where the Buchanan household gathered in the evening to enjoy piano music, conversation and reading. (Courtesy The James Buchanan Foundation for the Preservation of Wheatland.)

banister as the last piece of work done by the builder. According to legend, such a marker guaranteed peace and other blessings to the occupants of the new house. The winding stairway turns at the doorway steps to the guest bedroom, curves back to form a tiny balcony from which the first floor can be viewed, and then blends into the second floor of the house.

The old kitchen, with its great fireplace and large iron kettles, is typical of 19th-century home life. At Wheatland most of the food was prepared in a basement kitchen, then warmed and served from the first-floor room.

James Buchanan's bedroom has green woolen draperies and red upholstered furniture. A carved four-post bed is covered with an appliquéd quilt. A silk dressing gown is on view. A small dressing room contains a china bowl and pitcher set with all of the necessary accessories, as well as a shaving stand. The dark-paneled bathroom was an innovation in the 19th century, and the deep zinc-lined bathtub was considered a luxury by many people.

Buchanan is thought to have died in a small room in the west wing of Wheatland. It is a bright, comfortable room, with a fireplace and a view of the lawns from two sides. Plainly furnished at the time of his death, it was described as having a large calf-bound family Bible and two pieces of embroidery done by his mother when he was young.

The rear of Wheatland has a long veranda in the center and a small kitchen porch, which look out on large trees and a gently sloping lawn. Flower gardens and walks border these grounds. Buchanan often strolled to the woods on the high ground to the rear of the house to enjoy the view of the valley and rolling hills to the west. The rear grounds also contain an outhouse, an old pump on the original well site, a smokehouse and a large carriage house. Buchanan's restored carriage, built in 1853, may be seen here.

Buchanan died on June 1, 1868, at the age of seventy-seven, and was buried at Woodward Hill Cemetery in Lancaster.

14

Abraham Lincoln

THE BIRTHPLACE NEAR HODGENVILLE, KENTUCKY; THE
BOYHOOD HOME AT LINCOLN CITY, INDIANA; AND
THE FAMILY HOME IN SPRINGFIELD, ILLINOIS.

HOW TO GET THERE/WHEN TO VISIT

The **Lincoln birthplace,** administered by the National Park Service, is
about 3 miles south of Hodgenville, Kentucky, on U.S. 31E and Kentucky
61. Open daily from 8 A.M. to 6:45 P.M. from mid-June to Labor Day and to
4:45 P.M. the rest of the year. Closed December 25. No admission fee. Tel.:
(502) 358-3874.

The **boyhood home,** also administered by the National Park Service, is part
of the Lincoln Boyhood National Memorial, located on Indiana Highway
162, 4 miles south of Dale, Indiana. Visitor center open daily from 8 A.M. to
5 P.M. Closed Thanksgiving, Christmas and New Year's. Adult admission
fee of $1 ($3 maximum per family) is good for all attractions and activities.
Education groups, children 16 and under and seniors admitted free. Tel.:
(812) 937-4541.

The **family home** at the Lincoln Home National Historic Site, also
administered by the National Park Service, is located near the corner of 7th
Street and Capitol Avenue in Springfield, Illinois, and can be most easily
reached on the business bypass through Springfield from Interstate 55.
Open daily from 9 A.M. to 5 P.M. Closed Thanksgiving, Christmas and New
Year's. Admission is free. House tours by ticket only; these are free and
distributed on a first-come, first-served basis, except for organized groups,
which may reserve in advance. Tel.: (217) 492-4150.

AT THE CLOSE OF the Revolution, sometime between 1782 and 1784, the Lincoln
family moved from Virginia across the mountains to the frontier region of
Kentucky, then the outpost of pioneer advance into the wilderness and a bloody

The traditional birthplace cabin and home of Abraham Lincoln during about two and a half of his first years. The cabin stands within a memorial building on, or very near, the original site south of Hodgenville, Kentucky. Between 1860 and 1906 it was removed from and returned to this site several times. In 1906 the Lincoln Farm Association bought the cabin and in 1911 reerected it in its present location.

battleground for scattered settlements and isolated families. Here Abraham Lincoln, grandfather of the sixteenth President and the man for whom he was named, was killed by an Indian from ambush in May 1786. Thomas Lincoln, Abraham's son and the father of the future President, was then about eight years old.

Thomas Lincoln was a good-natured, honest man who always seemed to be retreating before the approach of the comforts and advantages of a developing community—as though they were foreign to his Spartan nature. About 1800 he settled in Elizabethtown, Kentucky, and became for a time a hardworking, industrious member of the community, acquiring a reputation as a good carpenter. On June 12, 1806, he married Nancy Hanks and made a home with her in Elizabethtown, where their first child, Sarah, was born in 1807.

On December 12, 1808, Thomas Lincoln bought for $200 in cash the 348-acre Sinking Spring farm a few miles south of Hodgen's Mill. He, his wife and their infant daughter moved into a one-room cabin near the limestone spring of cool water for which the place was named. It was in this cabin that Abraham Lincoln was born on February 12, 1809.

In March 1860 the remains of a log cabin on the Lincoln farm were removed to another farm a little over a mile to the north. The cabin remained there until 1895, when it was purchased by A. W. Dennett of New York and returned to the Lincoln farm where Dennett had purchased 110 acres. Several times during the following years the cabin was dismantled and the logs carefully marked and taken to various expositions around the country.

The Lincoln Farm Association, formed to raise funds to preserve the birthplace and establish a memorial to Lincoln, bought the cabin in 1906 and sent it to Louisville, where it was put in storage. In 1909 it was returned temporarily to the birthplace farm for the ceremonies attending the laying of the cornerstone of the memorial building by President Theodore Roosevelt. Upon completion of the building in 1911, the cabin was taken on the last of its travels back to the site of its origin and reerected within the memorial building.

The memorial building housing the cabin, designed by John Russell Pope, was built of Connecticut pink granite and Tennessee marble between 1909 and 1911. The birthplace cabin is part of a site that comprises 116 acres, nearly 100 of which were part of the original Thomas Lincoln farm. The site, administered by the National Park Service, includes the memorial building and the Sinking Spring. The area became a National Historic Site on September 8, 1959.

The memorial building, erected by the Lincoln Farm Association from funds obtained by popular subscription, mostly by American schoolchildren. Each of the fifty-six steps represents a year of Lincoln's life. Sixteen ceiling rosettes symbolize Lincoln as having been the sixteenth President of the United States.

The Sinking Spring. The Thomas Lincoln family obtained its water supply from this spring; the infant Abraham had his earliest drinks of water from this source. When Thomas Lincoln moved here in 1808, the 300-acre farm already was variously known as Sinking Spring, Rock Spring or Cave Spring Farm, taking its name from this spring.

At Lincoln Boyhood National Memorial, the Lincoln Living Historical Farm recreates pioneer life of the 1820s. The working farm features hewn-log buildings, such as the cabin, smokehouse, carpentry shop and stable. Fields and gardens roamed by a variety of farm animals set a scene in which young Abe Lincoln would feel right at home. (Courtesy Lincoln Boyhood National Memorial.)

The Lincolns lived about two and a half years at the Sinking Spring farm, which eventually was lost to them because of a defective land title. Before midsummer 1811 they moved to a farm on Knob Creek, where young Abe attended his first school. Threatened by another land suit in 1816, Thomas Lincoln decided to move to Indiana, where he could hold his land without fear of losing it. In December the family packed their belongings and started for the Ohio River at Anderson's Ferry. After crossing the river, they followed a wagon road twelve miles. The remaining distance to the land to which Lincoln had laid claim had to be hacked out by hand. Abraham was only seven, but he later remembered the trip to Little Pigeon Creek as one of the hardest experiences of his life.

It was winter, and some kind of shelter had to be put up. With the help of neighbors, Thomas cleared a spot on high ground and erected a cabin, finishing it in several weeks. Such a typical southwestern Indiana log cabin would measure about 18 by 20 feet in floor area and 8 feet from floor to rafters. The unhewn logs with bark were about 12 inches in diameter so eight such logs were required for each wall, plus a few more to fill in the gables.

Before the walls were built, four cornerstones were laid, with two side logs, hewn flat on one side, positioned on them. Properly notched logs were then used as covering and held in place, one on top of the next. Smaller poles were cut for the roof. Clapboards split from straight-grained logs were then used as covering and held in place by weighted poles extending the width of the roof. Openings for a door, one or two windows and a chimney were then cut. Finally a stick chimney was erected and the fireplace covered with stiff mud and daubed over the chinking on both the inside and outside of the cabin.

According to Dennis Hanks, a nineteen-year-old cousin who came to live with them in the fall of 1818, Thomas Lincoln's cabin was very crude. It contained one room with a loft above reached by pegs driven into the walls. The floor of the loft, where the children slept, was of clapboard, but there was only dirt on the cabin floor and no windows or door, not even the traditional deerskin hung before the entrance.

Autumn frosts of 1818 had already colored the foliage of the huge trees of oak, hickory and walnut when Nancy Hanks Lincoln became desperately ill. She was stricken with milk sickness, a poisoning caused by the plant white snakeroot. Cows ate this abundant weed and passed the poison on in their milk. On October 5, 1818, Nancy died.

A year later, Thomas Lincoln, unable to stand the loneliness without a helpmate, returned to Kentucky, where he married Sarah Bush Johnston on December 2, 1819. Upon her arrival at the Lincoln homesite she put Thomas Lincoln and Dennis Hanks to work renovating the cabin. Rough-hewn planks, called "puncheons," were cut and laid for flooring, the roof was finished, and a door hung. The cabin was cleansed, bedding put on the pole and clapboard beds, the fireplace overhauled, and ample cooking utensils installed. Thomas put together a table, a stool and a chair or two. Finally, the inside of the cabin was whitewashed.

During the winter when Abraham was eleven, he attended Andrew Crawford's subscription school. Two years later he attended infrequently a school taught by James Swaney. Then in his fifteenth year he attended Azel Dorsey's school. Dorsey was well trained, and Abraham probably received his best education there.

By his nineteenth year Abe had reached a height of six foot four and weighed nearly 190 pounds. People remembered that he could hoist more weight and drive an ax deeper than any man around.

Sometime in mid-1829, the Lincolns decided to leave Indiana for the fertile plains of Illinois. Piling their goods into three wagons, the Lincoln family drove slowly away from the homestead that had sheltered Abraham Lincoln for the thirteen formative years that saw Lincoln the boy grow to become Lincoln the man. Within a month the wagons reached the prairie country that would claim Abraham for his next thirty years.

The Lincoln Living Historical Farm is an operating reproduction of the kind of farmstead that Lincoln's father built in the Indiana wilderness. Using authentic methods and materials, "pioneers" demonstrate daily farming and domestic chores. (Courtesy Lincoln Boyhood National Memorial.)

A replica of the Lincoln boyhood home is part of the Lincoln Living Historical Farm at Lincoln City, Indiana. The Lincoln cabin is surrounded by an orchard and a garden. A smokehouse, corncrib and barn are close by, as well as a carpenter's shop housing various tools and implements important to a frontier family. Farm crops are planted in the garden by pioneer methods, and there are fields for cotton and tobacco. Visitors can leave the farm and walk to Nancy Lincoln's grave and the Memorial Visitor Center.

Lincoln arrived in Springfield in 1837 with all of his possessions in his saddlebags. Though he was a new resident he was not a stranger to the town. Since 1834, as a resident of the village of New Salem, he had represented Sangamon County in the Illinois General Assembly and helped move the capital from Vandalia to Springfield. The prairie city was growing rapidly and possessed opportunities that could only enhance the promising future of a young lawyer like Lincoln. Here he could meet politicians and local leaders from all over the state. One was Stephen A. Douglas, a state senator who defeated Lincoln in the 1858 election for the U.S. Senate and whom, among others, Lincoln defeated for the Presidency in 1860. And here Lincoln met Mary Todd, his wife to be.

Mary Todd came from a prominent family. She was born in Lexington, Kentucky, on December 13, 1818, the daughter of Robert Todd, president of the Lexington branch of the Bank of Kentucky. She was smart, high-strung, impulsive

Abraham Lincoln and son William Wallace Lincoln in front of their Springfield, Illinois, residence at Eighth and Jackson Streets in the summer of 1860. (Photograph by J. A. Whipple. Courtesy Chicago Historical Society.)

and vivacious, but at the same time willful and demanding, with a hair-trigger temper. They had met in 1837 and again in 1839, and within a year they had reached an understanding and were talking of marriage. After a tempestuous on-again-off-again-on-again courtship they married on the morning of November 4, 1842.

The Lincolns spent their first year of marriage in a hotel boardinghouse called the Globe Tavern. Here their first child, Robert Todd Lincoln, was born on August 1, 1843. He was the first of four sons and the only one to grow to manhood.

The Globe Tavern was a noisy, crowded place, so the Lincolns moved, spending the winter of 1843–44 in a rented three-room cottage at 214 South Fourth Street. The following spring Lincoln bought the home of Reverend Charles Dresser on the corner of Eighth and Jackson streets for $1200 in cash and a small lot worth $300. The house that Lincoln bought was originally built for the Reverend Dresser in the autumn of 1839, probably by his brother Henry. The Greek Revival house, one and a half stories high, had a frame of rough-sawed oak, with oak sills. Pine was used for the interior trim and doors, and the floors were made of random-width oak. Wooden pegs and hand-wrought nails were used in the construction.

In this house the other three Lincoln children were born: Edward Baker on March 10, 1846; William Wallace, December 21, 1850; and Thomas on April 4, 1853. Here, too, the couple's second son died in 1850.

In June 1850 Lincoln improved his front yard by the erection of a brick retaining wall and fence along the front of the fifty-foot lot. In June 1855 he had the brick wall and fence extended along one-fourth of the Jackson Street side of the lot.

From 1849 to 1854 Lincoln retired from political life and devoted his time to practicing law. These were among the most fruitful years of his life. He became a more skilled lawyer and grew to be widely respected for his power of lucid argument and almost fanatical honesty. In 1854, Lincoln once again turned toward politics, opposing the expansion of slavery. That year he was elected to the state legislature but soon resigned to run for the U.S. Senate as a Whig. He lost and turned again to his law practice, handling cases of increasing importance. He remained politically active, however, joining the new Republican Party in 1856.

In 1855, the Lincolns began a series of major improvements to the home. Springfield was becoming a city. Railroads linked it with Chicago and St. Louis and the Great Western Railroad extended its tracks from east to west across the state. Streets in the business district were covered with planking, and gaslights illuminated the downtown intersections.

In keeping with the trend, and to provide room for a family of growing boys, the Lincolns enlarged their home from a story and a half to two full stories. The work was done at a cost of $2700. The builders raised the roof of the front part of the house nine feet. Two-by-six pine studding was inserted and fastened to the existing rough-sawed oak studding of the original walls. When completed, the ceilings of the two half-story bedrooms at the front of the house had been raised to a height of eleven feet. The ceilings of the three first-floor rooms at the rear of the house were raised a foot, and an entire story (containing four rooms) was added above them, rounding out the house to a two-story dwelling. Mrs. Lincoln had two false fireplaces built in the two second-floor bedrooms. Neither was intended for use, but were to serve as a decorative background for the Franklin stoves.

Front parlor in the Lincoln residence in Springfield, late 1860 or early 1861. Photo is from an engraving in Frank Leslie's Illustrated Newspaper, *March 9, 1861.* (Courtesy Chicago Historical Society.)

In the Illinois senatorial campaign of 1858 two events made Lincoln a national figure: the Lincoln–Douglas debates and his speech to the Young Men's Central Republican Union of New York City at Cooper Union on February 27, 1860, when he said: "Let us have faith that right makes might, and in that faith let us, to the end, dare to do our duty as we understand it." At the 1860 Republication convention in Chicago, he received the nomination for President. He was elected on November 6. Three months later, Lincoln left for Washington, never to return to Springfield and the house on Eighth Street.

The house had to be vacated for a tenant, some household articles sold, others stored and others packed for use in the White House. In January the furniture was advertised for private sale. Lucian Tilton, president of the Great Western Railroad, to whom Lincoln rented the house, purchased some of the household effects. After Tilton vacated the house in 1869 and moved into a house on Oak Street in Chicago, the great Chicago fire of 1871 destroyed many of the Lincoln furnishings along with Tilton's house.

In 1954 the Lincoln home was restored by the state of Illinois, the Abraham Lincoln Association of Springfield and the National Society of the Colonial Dames of America in Illinois. In 1987–88 the home was again restored, this time by the National Park Service, at a cost of $2.2 million. It is now the focus of a four-square-block area that makes up the Lincoln Home National Historic Site, which also includes the homes of fourteen of the Lincolns' neighbors. Within walking distance are the Lincoln Depot, where, on the rainswept morning of February 11, 1861, the President said good-bye to his neighbors; the Old State Capitol; the Lincoln–Herndon Law Office; and the Illinois State Museums.

15

Andrew Johnson

THE BIRTHPLACE IN RALEIGH, NORTH CAROLINA;
AND THE HOMESTEAD IN GREENEVILLE, TENNESSEE.

HOW TO GET THERE/WHEN TO VISIT

The **Johnson birthplace** is located in Mordecai Historic Park at 1 Mimosa Street, between Mordecai Drive and Wake Forest Road, Raleigh. Open Tuesday through Friday from 10 A.M. to 2 P.M., and Saturday and Sunday from 2 P.M. to 4 P.M. No admission charge. Tel.: (919) 834-4844.

The **homestead,** part of the Andrew Johnson National Historic Site, is located on Main Street in Greeneville, and can be reached by U.S. 321 or U.S. 11E. Open daily, except Christmas Day, from 9 A.M. to 5 P.M. Admission is $1 for adults (age 17 and over); $3 maximum per family. Tel.: (615) 638-3551.

IN 1808, THE YEAR that Andrew Johnson was born, Raleigh, North Carolina, was a small town of less than one thousand inhabitants. Although the capital of the state, it was still only a country village.

Andrew's father and mother lived in a small house provided for the employees of Casso's Inn and on the inn property. His father was a hostler at the inn and also janitor of the State House, which was north of the inn. His mother did weaving for the inn and was known as "Polly the Weaver." This, then, was the proletarian environment into which Andrew Johnson was born. His parents, while poor and uneducated, were liked and respected by the townspeople.

In 1812 Johnson's father died of overexertion when he heroically rescued two friends from drowning. Andrew, age three, and his brother, William, were cared for by their mother until they were old enough to learn a trade. At the age of fourteen Andrew was apprenticed to James J. Selby, a tailor, whose clientele included the leading gentlemen of the community.

When Andrew was sixteen he got into trouble for throwing stones at the house of a Raleigh tradesman. The lady of the house threatened to have him and his cavorting friends arrested, and Andrew left in a hurry, taking his tailor's tools with him. He went to Carthage, sixty miles southwest of Raleigh, and set himself up as a tailor. But Carthage proved to be too close to Raleigh for comfort, so he went farther south to Laurens, South Carolina. Later Andrew returned to Raleigh to work out his apprenticeship with Selby, but Selby had sold his shop. So Andrew once again left Raleigh, this time with his mother, stepfather and brother, in a small wagon drawn by an old horse.

The birthplace, built about 1795, is a small two-story structure that has been restored to its probable appearance at the time of Johnson's birth. None of the present furnishings was actually owned by the Johnson family. The articles in the house are of the kind in common use during the early years of the 19th century and, as far as possible, are authentic items of that period.

The house in which Johnson was born originally stood on Fayetteville Street but was later moved to East Carrabus Street, then moved again to Pullen Park, when it was purchased by the Wake County Committee of the Colonial Dames of America and presented to the city of Raleigh. Finally, in 1975, it was moved to its present location in Mordecai Historic Park where it is now supported by Capital Area Preservation, Inc., a nonprofit organization, in cooperation with the city of Raleigh.

The birthplace of Andrew Johnson in Raleigh, North Carolina. Johnson's parents were poor and uneducated, and Johnson himself had no formal schooling, learning to read and write at the age of ten. He and his brother were raised in this house by their mother, the father having died when Andrew was three. (Courtesy North Carolina Museum of History.)

The furnishings in Johnson's birthplace are typical of the early 19th century, although they were not actually used by the Johnson family. These photos show parts of the kitchen. (Courtesy North Carolina Museum of History.)

At the age of seventeen Andrew had already become the accepted head of the family. His mother depended upon his judgment, and his stepfather (Turner Dougherty) was willing to do whatever he said. In the month of August 1826 the Johnsons sold or gave away what possessions they could not load on a cart and set out on the long and dusty westward path across the Smokies. After a month's travel over the Daniel Boone Trail, they reached the town of Greeneville, Tennessee, in September of 1826. Here Andrew, at the age of eighteen, set up a tailor shop of his own. In 1827 Johnson married Eliza McCardle, the ceremony being performed by Squire Mordecai Lincoln, a distant cousin of Abraham Lincoln. Eliza was well trained for this period and helped Andrew in his never-ceasing efforts to acquire an education. Ambitious and intelligent, she was to a great extent responsible for his success in business and for his entering an even more successful political career.

At the time of his marriage, Andrew's tailor shop was in the front room of a two-room building on Main Street in Greeneville. The back room served as kitchen, dining room, parlor and bedroom. The couple lived there until 1831, when they purchased a house on Water Street for a new home and a new shop. Between 1831 and 1843 the tailor shop was a busy place and it also became the center of village politics. The gathering place of local philosophers, it was the most talked-about establishment in east Tennessee. To keep himself posted on public affairs, Johnson employed a reader, paying him fifty cents a day to read aloud while he worked at the bench.

During these early days in Greeneville, Johnson formed close friendships with the people of the working class, who, in the spring of 1829, elected him alderman, an office to which he was reelected several times. He also served as mayor. Between 1829 and 1843 Johnson gave most of his time to activities such as the state constitutional convention of 1834, which abolished property qualifications for office seekers and imprisonment for debt and made a fuller guarantee of freedom of speech. He was increasingly recognized as a promising Democratic party leader.

From 1835 to 1843, Johnson served the state of Tennessee as representative (1835–37; 1839–41) and as senator (1841–43). In the Presidential campaign of 1840 he supported Van Buren. Although Van Buren was defeated, Johnson earned the reputation of being a capable political combatant, not only in east Tennessee but statewide. In 1843 the First Congressional District of Tennessee nominated him for the U.S. House of Representatives. He was elected and served in this body for ten years until 1853. Through capable oratory and by matching wits with the leading Whigs of the day, Johnson, the Democrat, was realizing a steady political growth. He was governor of Tennessee from 1853 to 1857 and a member of the U.S. Senate from 1857 to 1862.

After 1843 the tailor shop no longer played an important role in Johnson's life. Between 1843 and 1921 the tailor-shop building served for a time as a shop for another proprietor and later as a residence, but it always remained in the ownership of Johnson and his descendants. The Johnson home was erected by or for James Brannon, a brick mason in Greeneville, between 1849 and 1851. Johnson acquired the property on September 10, 1851, paying $950 in cash. There are no known records pertaining to the original construction of the Johnson home and there is only one known early picture, taken at the time of Johnson's death in 1875.

Architectural evidence shows that the original house of about 1850 consisted of a simple two-story brick block with a one-story ell extending toward the rear with six rooms above ground and two rooms of a semibasement nature. The house was set directly upon the street after the northern Irish fashion common to early Greeneville, Jonesboro and other related settlements. The house was entered through a central hall flanked by a room on either side, with chimneys at the ends. The same plan was repeated in the second-story portion of the block. The ell, two steps lower than the first floor of the main block, extended to a depth of two rooms toward the rear. These two rooms were separated by a chimney wall. There was a

Andrew Johnson's home in Greeneville, Tennessee, which was built around 1849–50 and purchased by Johnson in 1851, and was his home until he died in 1875. Today it is part of the enlarged Andrew Johnson National Historic Site, which includes the tailor shop Johnson lived and worked in during his early years in Greeneville, and the cemetery in which Johnson and his family are buried. (Courtesy Andrew Johnson National Historic Site.)

porch along the northeastern side of the ell, corresponding to the central stair hall, and this porch wrapped around the end of the ell. The only communication between the kitchen in the basement and the dining room above it was obviously by means of an outside stair. The house which Congressman Johnson bought in 1851 thus consisted of eight rooms disposed on three levels.

Around 1869–70, a second story to the ell and a large porch at the rear were added by Johnson. This addition was made during a period when Johnson had major repairs done on the entire house. The home had been occupied by Confederate forces and used as a dispensary or lying-in station for Confederate troops, and it was occupied as late as 1868 by Federal troops.

Johnson served as the seventeenth President from 1865 to 1869. His administration was marred by the impeachment proceedings against him, instigated by a hostile Congress and defeated by a single vote. A measure of vindication was realized for Johnson when in 1874 he was elected to the U.S. Senate. Complete vindication, however, waited until some fifty years after his death, when the Supreme Court ruled unconstitutional "The Tenure of Office Act," the defiance of which led to the impeachment attempt.

Johnson died July 31, 1875, leaving an estate estimated at $200,000. A complicated litigation ensued, and its wasn't until 1884 that his daughter, Martha, acquired possession of the Johnson homestead. In 1885 the house was completely remodeled. Victorian styling was achieved by the addition of gables over the front of the house and the southern flank of the second-story ell. A metal roof was installed; eaves were finished with deep wooden cornices; elaborate wooden pediments were applied over the old wooden lintels of the façade; some windows were lengthened to the floor; the roof line of the existing double-deck veranda was altered; a porch was added on the southwest side of the house; and the wall of one room was replaced by a large window extending onto the new porch. The interior was modernized. Martha's product was a handsome Victorian house. It soon became a public shrine.

Descendants continued to make additional changes. The grounds of the homestead were enlarged and built over, reaching its present size, 219 feet on Main Street and 187 feet on Water (College) Street, in the early years of Andrew Patterson's (Johnson's grandson's) ownership. Two frame houses were built north of the Johnson House; one was purchased south of the house, and three small houses were built on the Water Street frontage, making a total of seven rentals (including the tailor shop) plus the Johnson home now occupying the enlarged Andrew Johnson homestead.

The Johnson house looks today as it did in the period 1869–75, after Johnson had made his additions. Every room has furniture either used by the Johnsons or having a Johnson connection. Personal mementos include the tilt-top table with 500 pieces of inlaid wood presented to the Johnsons by the people of Ireland, and a hand-carved ivory basket presented to Mrs. Johnson by Queen Emma of the Hawaiian Islands. The cemetery in which Andrew Johnson is buried is dominated by a stately marble shaft rising some 26 feet and crowned by an Amerian eagle poised for flight.

Tailor, alderman, mayor, governor, congressman, senator, Vice-President and President—so ran the career of this man lauded as "The People's Friend." The three separate areas that make up the Andrew Johnson National Historic Site in Greeneville reflect the three primary aspects of this distinguished career: the tailor shop, symbol of his humble origin, where he worked during his early manhood and also a house in which he lived from around 1838 to 1851; the homestead, representing his unaffected attitudes about unpretentious living, especially significant when viewed from the vantage point of what he could have afforded in the later years of his political success; and the cemetery with its towering monument, testimony to the respect and admiration of the people he served.

16

Ulysses S. Grant

THE BIRTHPLACE AT POINT PLEASANT, OHIO;
THE HOME IN GALENA, ILLINOIS; AND THE
COTTAGE NEAR SARATOGA SPRINGS, NEW YORK.

HOW TO GET THERE/WHEN TO VISIT

The **Grant birthplace** is located about 27 miles east of Cincinnati at the intersection of Routes 232 and 52. Open from April 1 to November 1 from 9:30 A.M. to noon and from 1 P.M. to 5 P.M. Adults pay 50 cents. Children under 12, free with parents, 25 cents by themselves.

The **Grant home,** on the U. S. Grant State Historic Site at 500 Bouthillier Street, Galena, can be reached by U.S. 20 and Illinois 84. Open daily from 9 A.M. to 5 P.M. Closed Thanksgiving, Christmas and New Year's days. Admission free. Tel.: (815) 777–3310.

The **Grant Cottage State Historic Site** can be reached by following the signs out of the town of Wilton on U.S. 9 north of Saratoga Springs. Open Wednesday through Sunday from 10 A.M. to 4 P.M., from the Memorial Day weekend through the Labor Day weekend. Admission is $2 for adults, $1.50 for seniors and $1 for children. Tel.: (518) 587–8277.

ULYSSES S. GRANT, THE eighteenth President, was born on April 27, 1822, in a little frame cottage near the Ohio River in the village of Point Pleasant, Ohio, some twenty-five miles upstream from Cincinnati. His father, Jesse Grant, and mother, Hannah Simpson Grant, had married the previous June, just a year after Jesse had arrived in Point Pleasant to work in a tannery. His mother, twenty-three years old when Ulysses was born, was the daughter of a well-to-do farmer in the region. After their marriage the couple settled next to the tannery in a one-story, two-room house.

The house was built in 1817 of white Allegheny pine, and the main part measures 16 by 19½ feet. It has a steep roof—a pitch of 5 feet. On the outside of the north end is a huge chimney servicing a spacious fireplace. The front end of the house faces Indian Creek. There is a door on each side. The interior contains a kitchen, a living room and, at the south end, the bedroom in which Grant was born.

The birthplace of Ulysses S. Grant in Point Pleasant, Ohio, a village on the Ohio River. The family lived here only a year after Grant's birth, moving to a farm in 1823. (Courtesy Ohio Historical Society.)

Living room in Grant's birthplace. (Courtesy Ohio Historical Society.)

After Grant's birth, his parents remained at Point Pleasant for about a year, moving to a farm near Georgetown, Ohio, in 1823.

When Ulysses S. Grant and his family, having been barely able to eke out a meager living in St. Louis by farming and real-estate dealings, arrived in Galena, Illinois, by steamboat in the spring of 1860, the city had already begun its economic decline. Galena had experienced boom-town prosperity from the lead mines in the 1820s and become a bustling Mississippi River port and ambitious mercantile center in the 1840s.

Grant had hoped to reverse his economic misfortunes by moving to northwest Illinois. In Galena he worked as a clerk and traveling salesman for a leather goods store owned by his father and operated by his brothers, Simpson and Orvil. Until he left Galena in the spring of 1861 to serve in the Civil War, Grant and his family rented a modest brick house on the west side of the river.

On August 18, 1865, Galena greeted the return of its victorious general with a grand celebration. There was a jubilant procession, decorated arches, speeches and a holiday atmosphere. From a triumphal arch spanning Main Street, thirty-six young ladies dressed in white waved American flags and threw bouquets. During the ceremonies, a small group of citizens of Galena presented a furnished house on Bouthillier Street to the General.

Grant home in Galena, Illinois, on Bouthillier Street. Built in 1859–60 in the "Italianate Bracketed" style, it was given to Grant in 1865 by some of the town's citizens upon his triumphant return after the Civil War. (Photo by James Quick. Courtesy Illinois Historic Preservation Agency.)

Dining room, containing silver used by the Grants in the White House and Grant family china. (Photo by James Quick. Courtesy Illinois Historic Preservation Agency.)

Parlor in the Grant home at Galena, where Grant learned he had been elected President in 1868. The Brussels carpet is an exact replica of the original. The furniture belonged to the Grant family. (Photo by James Quick. Courtesy Illinois Historic Preservation Agency.)

Kitchen, Grant home. (Courtesy Illinois Historic Preservation Agency.)

General Grant and his family left for Washington, D.C., on September 12, 1865, where he continued his duties as commanding general of the army. Like most of his later trips, this visit was relatively short. The Grants returned to Galena in the fall of 1868 and remained there throughout his successful campaign for the Presidency.

During the next fifteen years the Grant family used their Galena home as a haven during the course of campaigns and long journeys. The General enjoyed these brief periods, renewing old friendships in Galena and the surrounding area.

Grant served two terms as President, from 1868 to 1876. Aferward he and his family embarked in May 1877 on a trip around the world, during which they were received by dignitaries in all the countries they visited. Returning to San Francisco in September 1879, the Grants made a triumphant journey to Galena. Their arrival "home" on November 5 prompted a large civic reception and celebration. Leaving in December, the General and his family returned to Galena only for short visits in 1880. President Grant left for New York City in September 1880 and never stayed in his Galena house again, even though he and his wife visited Galena for the last time in May 1883. On July 23, 1885, Grant died at Mount McGregor, New York.

The Grant home is a brick house in the "Italianate Bracketed" style of the period, elements of which include the well-defined rectilinear blocks of the building; the projecting or overhanging eaves supported by brackets; the low-pitched roof; the piazza, or covered porch; and the balustraded balcony. It was designed by William Dennison and constructed in 1859–60 as a residence for Alexander J. Jackson of Galena.

The original plans and specifications were available for guidance during its restoration in 1955–57. At this time the home was strengthened internally to

Workroom, with sewing machine and unique wallpaper of the period. (Courtesy Illinois Historic Preservation Agency.)

General and Mrs. Grant's bedroom. (Photo by James Quick. Courtesy Illinois Historic Preservation Agency.)

Another bedroom in the Grant home. (Photo by James Quick. Courtesy Illinois Historic Preservation Agency.)

accommodate the many visitors. The original specifications state that "The House is to be of brick, of 36 feet by 40 feet, to be two stories, each to be 11 feet clear stud. There is to be an addition on the back of 30 feet by 17 feet, one story high, of 9 feet high clear height."

The furniture in the house today was largely owned by the Grant family in 1865, with additions made during restoration to make the house characteristic of the Victorian 1870s. In the spacious parlor displaying the old horsehair-covered parlor set, a new loop Brussels carpet shows the exact colors and patterns of the worn original. In all rooms actual old ingrain or Brussels carpet might have known the footsteps of the Grants, while period wallpapers grace the walls as they would have over a hundred years ago. In the dining room the table is set with china and silver used by the Grants in the White House, while souvenirs and trophies from the trip around the world furnish intimate touches to every room. In Mrs. Grant's bedroom can be seen an old pair of shoes with her name and that of the maker printed in gold inside the sole.

Grant's home stands in historically preserved Galena. Also to be seen is the old Grant Leather Store, Grant's home on High Street, before the war, and other historic houses.

A corner of Grant's library, showing memorabilia and a bust of Grant. (Courtesy Illinois Historic Preservation Agency.)

Another bedroom. (Photo by James Quick. Courtesy Illinois Historic Preservation Agency.)

Cottage on Mt. McGregor near Saratoga Springs, New York, where Grant, suffering from throat cancer, came in June of 1885 hoping that the mountain air might help relieve his condition. He lived here about six weeks, dying on July 23, 1885. (Courtesy Division for Historic Preservation Files.)

Ten miles north of Saratoga Springs, at the summit of Mount McGregor, the New York State Office of Parks, Recreation and Historic Preservation, Bureau of Historic Sites, and the Saratoga County Historical Society maintain Grant Cottage, a simple little structure to which President Grant came in June 1885, suffering from a cancerous throat condition.

The cottage was then owned by the Drexel family of New York City. They gladly made it available to General Grant, whose physician hoped that the invigorating mountain air might prove beneficial to his famous patient. In that day, Saratoga Springs (with which the mountain had a rail connection) was at the peak of its popularity as a health resort and social center.

General Grant occupied the cottage for six weeks. During these last days he finished writing his *Personal Memoirs,* although the condition of his throat frequently prevented dictation to his secretary. It was his last act of heroism in a losing battle.

To fit the cottage, formerly used as a boarding house, for the General's visit, the owners had it repapered, repainted and refurnished throughout. The fireplace in the reception room was also constructed at this time.

Interior of Grant cottage. The furnishings are as they were when Grant died. (Courtesy Division for Historic Preservation Files.)

Early photo of Grant cottage interior, with display paying homage to the General. Grant is buried in New York City. (Courtesy Division for Historic Preservation Files.)

General Grant died there on July 23, 1885. After his death his body was put aboard the heavily draped funeral train and taken to Albany, where the casket rested overnight in the main corridor of the State Capitol. Today this spot is marked by a brass plate in the floor. From there the casket was taken to New York City.

The simple furnishings of the cottage—the bed, chairs and tables—remain as they were when General Grant died. Personal belongings, not removed at the time, have been on exhibit since 1890. From the "Lookout," to which General Grant was sometimes wheeled in his chair, one can still view and enjoy the vast panorama of fields, rolling hills and distant mountains to the east.

17
Rutherford B. Hayes

HIS HOME IN FREMONT, OHIO.

HOW TO GET THERE/WHEN TO VISIT

Leave the Ohio Turnpike at Exit 6 for Fremont. The entrance to the **Hayes site** is at 1337 Hayes Avenue. The home is open from 12 noon to 5 P.M. Sundays and holidays (closed Thanksgiving, Christmas and New Year's days) and from 9 A.M. to 5 P.M. Monday to Saturday. The memorial is open from 9 A.M. to 5 P.M. daily and from 1:30 P.M. to 5 P.M. Sundays and holidays. Admission is $3 for adults, $1 for children (under 7 years old, free). Special group and senior citizens' rates provided upon request. Tel.: (419) 332-2081.

RUTHERFORD B. HAYES, THE nineteenth President, was born in Delaware, Ohio, on October 4, 1822, two months after the death of his father. He was reared by his mother, Sophia, with the help of her bachelor brother, Sardis Birchard. Hayes attended the public schools in Delaware; a Methodist academy in Norwalk, Ohio; and then the school of Isaac Webb in Middletown, Connecticut. He went to Kenyon College (1838–42), where he graduated as valedictorian. After a year studying law in Columbus, he attended Harvard Law School and was admitted to the Ohio Bar in 1845.

He began his practice of law in Lower Sandusky (now Fremont), where his uncle Sardis had been living since 1827. After four years in the village, he moved, in 1850, to Cincinnati, then the largest city in the West. Within six or seven years he had made a sufficient name for himself to be appointed city solicitor. When the Civil War broke out, Governor William Dennison appointed him a major in the Ohio volunteers; he served with the 23rd Regiment of Ohio Infantry throughout the war. He was wounded four times, once seriously, and prior to his resignation from the service was brevetted a major general for "gallant and distinguished service during the campaign of 1864 in West Virginia and particularly in the battles of Fisher's Hill and Cedar Creek, Virginia."

In 1864 Hayes was elected to Congress even though he refused to leave the battlefield to campaign. After the war he served his term and was reelected. In 1867 he resigned as congressman to run successfully for governor of Ohio. He served two terms, 1868–72, and returned for a third term in 1876. That year he became the

The home of Rutherford B. Hayes at Spiegel Grove in Fremont, Ohio. Built in 1859–60 by Sardis Birchard, Hayes's uncle and legal guardian, it was occupied by the Hayes family in 1873. With the exception of his term in the White House, Hayes lived here until his death in 1893. (Courtesy Rutherford B. Hayes Library.)

Republican candidate for the Presidency, running against Governor Samuel J. Tilden of New York. After an exciting campaign, in which he did not participate personally, and a contested election declared by a special electoral commission created by Congress, Hayes was announced the winner and elected President just three days before the inauguration on March 5, 1877.

Hayes concluded the Federal government's postwar reconstruction of the South by removing the army from Florida, Louisiana and South Carolina and by restoring local self-government. He initiated strong civil-service reforms, paving the way for a permanent civil-service program, and he strengthened the national currency by resuming payments in gold for paper money.

After his Presidency, Hayes returned to Fremont and devoted the remaining years of his life to philanthropic enterprises such as the education of black people in the South, a national program for manual training, improvements and reforms of prisons and the rehabilitation of criminals, and matters pertaining to war veterans.

The site of Spiegel Grove, the home of Rutherford B. Hayes, was selected by his uncle Sardis. The deep woods, cool shade and pools reminded Sardis of the German

The large drawing room of the Hayes home, showing a life-size portrait of Hayes, mahogany period furniture and a Chinese rug. (Courtesy Rutherford B. Hayes Library.)

Library in the Hayes home. President Hayes's personal library, which included thousands of volumes of American history—practically everything that was available up to his death—has been removed to the fireproof memorial building known as the Hayes Library and Museum. The shelves in this room have been refilled with volumes of general literature, giving it the appearance it had when Hayes used it as an office. (Courtesy Rutherford B. Hayes Library.)

President and Mrs. Hayes's bedroom, showing old mahogany furniture and a four-poster bed. The pictures are of Mrs. Hayes. Both Hayes and his wife died in this room. (Courtesy Rutherford B. Hayes Library.)

fairy tales of his youth. He selected it with the intention of spending his declining years with Hayes and his family. The house was started on August 22, 1859, and Hayes came to Fremont with his family to live with his uncle in 1873. Hayes took over the Spiegel Grove property and added an office, a kitchen and a library to house his large book collection. In 1874, Sardis Birchard died.

In 1880, President Hayes, ready to return to Fremont from the White House, remodeled the interior and added a large section to the north, duplicating the original gabled brick front of the house. In 1889 the current large dining room, the kitchen and several upstairs bedrooms were added. Only two rooms of the original house remained after both of these renovations. They were the red parlor and the ancestral room where Sardis Birchard had slept.

When he was President, Hayes began naming trees in Spiegel Grove in honor of important guests at the grove. This custom is still observed today. Hayes also arranged the walks and driveways and planted trees and shrubs. It was a happy home where children gathered frequently and many guests were entertained.

Mrs. Hayes died there in June 1889 and the ex-President followed her in death in January 1893.

Spiegel Grove is on a wooded 25 acres that encompass a nearly half-mile section of the historic Sandusky-Scioto Indian trail. The site consists of the Hayes home, the Hayes Library and Museum, and Hayes's tomb. The six entrances are enhanced by impressive iron gates which protected the White House grounds in Washington,

D.C., before and during the Hayes administration. The house, meticulously furnished, was opened to the public in 1966.

The library, in addition to more than 100,000 volumes, contains a large collection of personal items of President Hayes, Mrs. Hayes and their children: correspondence, diaries, scrapbooks, photographs, paintings, etc. Hayes's personal library of local and American history is housed here.

The museum exhibits portray the lives and contributions of President and Mrs. Hayes, the Presidency and America in their time. They include Mrs. Hayes's reception gowns, a carved sideboard, state china, the Presidential carriage and Fanny Hayes's dollhouse, among other family exhibits. There are original letters written and signed by all the Presidents of the United States from the time of George Washington to the present. There are personal objects associated with Abraham Lincoln, including a pair of his gloves, a desk he used, slippers and an original handbill of Ford's Theatre for the performance on the night he was assassinated. There are also many relics of the American Indians, a fine weapons collection, Chinese curios and thousands of items gathered from all parts of the world.

18

James A. Garfield

LAWNFIELD, HIS HOME IN MENTOR, OHIO.

HOW TO GET THERE/WHEN TO VISIT

Lawnfield is located on U.S. Route 20 in Mentor, Ohio, between Painesville and Willoughby. It is open from 10 A.M. to 5 P.M. on Tuesday through Saturday and from 12 noon to 5 P.M. on Sunday. It is closed Easter, Thanksgiving, Christmas and New Year's days. Admission is $3 for adults, $2 for seniors (age 60 and over), $1.50 for children 6–12, and free for children under 6. Tel.: (216) 255-8722.

JAMES A. GARFIELD WAS born on November 19, 1831, in a log cabin in Orange Township, Cuyahoga County, Ohio. His father, a frontier farmer, died before he was two years old. He and his two sisters and a brother, all older than he, were raised by a brave mother. He obtained his elementary education in a district school. Disliking farm work, he left home at sixteen and worked briefly driving horses on the tow path of the Ohio Canal. At seventeen he attended the Geauga Seminary at Chesterland, Ohio, having resolved to obtain a decent education and to become a teacher. At the seminary, he received his early religious training, and there he met Lucretia Rudolph, whom he married in 1858.

A taste of higher education sharpened his intellectual appetite and he went on to the Western Reserve Eclectic Institute, at Hiram, Ohio, and Williams College. He earned his way by doing carpentry work and teaching in nearby communities during the summer. Upon graduation he returned to the institute as professor of ancient languages and literature, and within a year became its principal. He was on its board of trustees (it became Hiram College in 1867) from 1864 until his death, and Lucretia, his wife, was on the same board from 1882 to 1897.

Early in the Civil War, Garfield served as a colonel and as a brigadier general. In 1863 he resigned from the army, at the request of President Lincoln, to assume his seat in the House of Representatives to which he had been elected the previous year. On his resignation he was promoted to major general in recognition of his distinguished service.

As a member of Congress he distinguished himself by his effective committee

Lawnfield, home of James A. Garfield in Mentor, Ohio. Garfield bought the house in 1876 and campaigned for President in 1880 from the front porch. (Courtesy Lake County Historical Society, Mentor, Ohio.)

service and as an orator. In 1876 he became the leader of the Republican party in the House, and in 1880 he was elected U.S. senator from Ohio.

That same year he was chosen by John Sherman to present Sherman's name for President at the Republican convention at Chicago. A three-way deadlock between Sherman, Blaine and Grant was broken on the thirty-sixth ballot when the delegates turned to Garfield as the one man behind whom the convention could unite.

Garfield campaigned from the front porch of Lawnfield, the home he bought and enlarged in 1876; it was probably the first and certainly one of the most successful "front porch" campaigns ever staged. At the northeast corner of the house is a small one-story building used in 1880 as the campaign office. There the telegrapher sent and received messages, and there Garfield received the news of his election as the twentieth President.

Garfield served for less than a year. He was shot by an assassin on July 2, 1881. He died on September 19, 1881, and was succeeded by Vice-President Chester Alan Arthur.

Left: Reception room fireplace at Lawnfield, one of twelve in the house. (Courtesy Lake County Historical Society.) *Right: First-floor bedroom occupied by Eliza Ballou Garfield, mother of the President.* (Courtesy Lake County Historical Society.)

Left: Bedroom of Garfield's daughter "Mollie." The Garfields had seven children in all. (Courtesy Lake County Historical Society.) *Right: Parlor at Lawnfield. The dark brown velvet gown was worn by Mrs. Garfield to teas in Washington.* (Courtesy Lake County Historical Society.)

Lawnfield was donated to the Western Reserve Historical Society to be opened as a public site in 1936. The first two floors of the mansion are filled with the original family furnishings. One can see the desk that Garfield used while principal of Western Reserve Eclectic Institute, the lunch basket he carried while traveling, the cradle made in 1832 for Mrs. Garfield by her father, dresses worn by Mrs. Garfield in the White House, and the President's clothes and canes. The memorial library, finished in distinctive hand-carved white oak, contains the desk Garfield used for

Left: Garfield's desk which he used as a congressman, now in a bay window of the memorial library at Lawnfield. (Courtesy Lake County Historical Society.) *Right: Portrait by Caroline Ransom of Garfield as a major general in the Union Army.*

seventeen years while a member of the United States House of Representatives. Also on display in the library is a stained-glass fire-screen portrait and a marble bust of the President.

The Civil War weapons used by General Garfield, the Bible he used for taking the oath as President of the United States, and the inaugural address in his own handwriting are exhibited on the first floor. There are original oil paintings and watercolors on the walls. There are twelve fireplaces, all different. Among the many furnishings and artifacts are Persian rugs, Royal Doulton and Wedgwood china, a tall Chinese rose medallion vase, gas chandeliers, kerosene lamps and the Haviland china used in the White House.

Immediately surrounding the home are over a hundred beautiful trees of many varieties, exotic as well as native, most of which were planted by the President and Mrs. Garfield. Also on the grounds is a furnished log-cabin replica of Garfield's frontier birthplace. Since 1988 the house and grounds have been the property of the National Park Service.

19

Chester A. Arthur

REPLICA OF THE CHILDHOOD HOME AT
NORTH FAIRFIELD, VERMONT.

HOW TO GET THERE/WHEN TO VISIT

The replica of the **Arthur childhood home** at the President Arthur Historic
Site is about 3½ miles east of Fairfield Station on the road that leads to State
Route 108. Open from Memorial Day to Columbus Day, Wednesday to
Sunday from 9:30 A.M. to 5:30 P.M. Closed Monday and Tuesday. There is no
admission charge, but donations are welcomed.

CHESTER ALAN ARTHUR, BORN on October 5, 1829, in North Fairfield, Vermont,
was our twenty-first President. His father, the Reverend William Arthur, Irish born,
came to Vermont from Canada in 1822 at the age of eighteen. He was converted to
the Baptist faith and preached in Vermont communities including North Fairfield.
He was interested in antiquarian research, published a work on family names, and
for several years edited *The Antiquarian*. In addition to being a clergyman he was
for a time principal of the academy at Williston, Vermont. Because of his father's
influence, Chester himself became a teacher during his younger years.

From 1845 to 1848 Chester attended Union College when his family moved to
Greenwich, New York, not far from Saratoga. He graduated with honors at the age
of eighteen. While at school he taught at Schaghticoke to help pay for his tuition,
which was $28 plus $125 for room and board. In 1851 Arthur was principal of an
academy in North Pownal, Vermont, where, three years later, James A. Garfield
taught penmanship.

Soon after 1851 Arthur began the study of law in Lansingbury, New York. He
then went to New York City, where, in 1853, he entered the law office of E. A. Culver
and had moderate success from the very first.

Coming of age at the precise time when both great political parties had declared
that thereafter there should be no agitation of the slavery question, he and his firm
attained much notoriety as legal companions of black people, and in 1856
succeeded in obtaining for them the right to ride in public conveyances. When the
Republican party was formed he was active in local organization.

Replica of the childhood home at the President Chester A. Arthur Historic Site in North Fairfield, Vermont. (Courtesy Vermont Division for Historic Preservation.)

On October 29, 1859, he married Ellen Louise Herndon of Fredericksburg, Virginia. They had three children, one of whom died in infancy. In 1860, when Edwin D. Morgan was reelected governor of New York, he appointed Arthur engineer-in-chief on his staff with the rank of brigadier general. In 1861 Arthur opened a branch quartermasters' department in New York City, becoming acting quartermaster general. Soon afterwards he had charge of preparing and equipping the soldiers of New York to be ready for President Lincoln's call. In February 1862 he was appointed inspector general. In December 1863, when Horatio Seymore became governor, the Democrats were in the ascendancy and Arthur returned to the practice of law.

For ten years he worked quietly in private and public duties until November 20, 1871, when he was appointed by President Grant to be collector of the port of New York, a post he held until suspended by President Hayes in July 1878, a casualty of Hayes's reform of "spoils system" abuses. He was then offered a consulship in Paris, which he declined. In 1879 he was elected chairman of the Republican state committee and in 1880 he was a delegate to the Republican national convention in Chicago, where he worked for the nomination of Grant. When, on the thirty-sixth ballot, General Garfield was nominated by a combination of Blaine and other anti-Grant delegates, the nomination of Arthur for Vice-President was made unanimous to conciliate the defeated Grant faction.

Arthur took the oath of office in New York City and was inaugurated on September 22, 1881, three days after President Garfield died of the wounds inflicted two months earlier by a disgruntled office seeker.

Arthur's administration was conservative and conciliatory. He began the reconstruction of the navy. He introduced the initial legislation for the discontinuance of extensive repairs to old wooden ships and the beginning of the construction of modern steel ships and guns. He also pressed for a more active participation in foreign trade by American ships. The United States Tariff Commission was instituted during his administration, and he introduced the civil service system.

He died in New York City on November 18, 1886, and was buried in Albany, New York, Rural Cemetery.

The exact location of the birthplace of Chester Arthur is unknown. In 1953 the state of Vermont reconstructed, on its original site, the house into which the Arthur family had moved when Chester was three months old. An old photograph of this house gives some indication of its shape and size. The replica was placed on a twenty-acre site in North Fairfield, Vermont. The replica was once thought to be of the birthplace (as seen on the plaque in the photograph), but this error has been corrected.

20

Benjamin Harrison

HIS HOME IN INDIANAPOLIS, INDIANA.

HOW TO GET THERE/WHEN TO VISIT

The **Harrison home** is located at 1230 North Delaware Street in Indianapolis, near the Meridian Street and Pennsylvania Street exits of I-65. If you choose public transport, take a No. 19 or No. 2 bus on Monument Circle and ask the driver to announce Delaware and 13th Streets. The home is open Monday through Saturday from 10 A.M. to 4 P.M. and Sunday from 12:30 P.M. to 4 P.M. It is closed Easter, Thanksgiving and Christmas. Phone for January hours. Adult admission is $2, students and children, $1. Special rates for prearranged group tours. Tel.: (317) 631-1898.

THE HARRISON FAMILY IS extraordinary in that for generation after generation it has produced national figures prominent in our history. Benjamin Harrison, the twenty-third President, was the great-grandson of Benjamin Harrison of Virginia, who signed the Declaration of Independence; the grandson of William Henry Harrison, ninth President and famed general; and the son of John Scott Harrison, a congressman.

After graduation from a Cincinnati law school, Harrison moved to Indianapolis in 1854 and established a prosperous law practice. When the Civil War broke out he entered the Union Army as a lieutenant and was soon promoted to colonel. The leader of the Indiana Regiment, he fought at Atlanta and at Nashville and was a brigadier general at the close of the war.

After an unsuccessful bid for governor in 1876, he was elected to the U.S. Senate in 1880. He was a noted advocate of civil service reform at a time when most party leaders preferred the patronage system. Defeated in the election of 1886, he left Washington, never expecting to return. Two years later, however, he was nominated for the Presidency and defeated Grover Cleveland in a close race. Cleveland won more popular votes, but Harrison captured the majority in the Electoral College.

During four years in the White House, he was noted for launching the construction of a modern navy, pioneering the conservation movement, promoting

Home of Benjamin Harrison in Indianapolis, Indiana. Built in 1874, it was Harrison's home until his death.

increased civil-service reform and establishing reciprocal trade agreements with many countries in Europe and Latin America.

Defeated by Cleveland in 1892, Harrison returned to Indianapolis to resume a successful law practice and to write a book, *This Country of Ours*, about the organization of the U.S. government. He died there on March 13, 1901.

The Harrison home, built in the spring of 1874, is a comfortable, well-built brick house of sixteen rooms. With the exception of the years Harrison spent in Washington as United States senator and President, he lived there continuously until his death in 1901. From this home he conducted one gubernatorial, two senatorial and two Presidential campaigns.

It is a rambling house. In the front parlor are large mirrors, delicate gold furniture, a crystal chandelier and an imported handmade rug, typical of the elegance of Victorian furnishings in Harrison's day.

The front hall contains the old cherry grandfather clock that was purchased from the Virginia branch of the Harrison family when Benjamin Harrison was senator. It was made about 1800 and has a moon dial.

A graceful half-spiral staircase, unsupported from the second to the third floors, leads to the third floor. Displayed here are campaign pictures, badges and changing exhibits. The back parlor has red velvet-covered inlaid walnut furniture that blends with the inlaid walnut mantels. The room was also used as a music room; the piano, in the corner to the right of the mantel, is of rosewood inlaid with mother of pearl, and with unusual round-tipped keys. There is a landscape which hung in the Harrison sitting room in the White House and an American-made music box popular in music and drawing rooms of that period.

In the library hang portraits of the last four of the illustrious Harrisons. Here are his desk and study table. The two upholstered chairs are original. There is also a Texas-steer-horn chair, an inaugural gift from a ranch owner in Texas, its seat covered in the original leopard skin. The cathedral chairs came from the homes of Indiana governors whose history is tied in with the Harrisons. The large, handsome, hand-carved walnut bookcase has never been moved from the library since being placed there in 1874. In it are Harrison's books, many autographed. The portrait of Lincoln, painted by Jacob Cox, hung at the head of Lincoln's casket April 30, 1865, the day his body lay in state in the old Indianapolis State House.

The furniture in the dining room is all original. Pitchers, goblets, vases, etc., are all inaugural gifts. The china closet houses many dishes of value and interest, among them pieces of Lincoln and Harrison Presidential china.

Harrison's law office is in a small room on the second floor. Here is the original furniture from his law office, located in the old Union Trust Building on East Market Street. Here also are two unusual filing cabinets and his own personal desk.

Left: A portion of the back parlor of the Benjamin Harrison home, showing the inlaid walnut mantel. (Photography by William B. Stewart.) *Right: The library in the Benjamin Harrison home. The bookcase and books belonged to Harrison.* (Photograph by William B. Stewart.)

A section of the Harrison dining room. (Photograph by William B. Stewart.)

The guest room has an interesting half-tester top bed used in this room during the 1870s. There are three Currier prints of William Henry Harrison and a portrait of Mrs. William Henry Harrison. The cradle was used by six of their children.

Next to the master bedroom is the upstairs sitting room, where the first Mrs. Harrison liked to paint. One of her paintings is displayed here. The second Mrs. Harrison used to entertain her lady friends in this room.

The master bedroom contains the massive hand-carved bed in which Benjamin Harrison died in this room. A dresser, rocker and two straight chairs complete a matched set. All the furniture is original.

21

Theodore Roosevelt

THE BIRTHPLACE IN NEW YORK CITY; AND THE HOME
AT SAGAMORE HILL, OYSTER BAY, LONG ISLAND, NEW YORK.

HOW TO GET THERE/WHEN TO VISIT

The **Theodore Roosevelt birthplace** at 28 East 20th Street, Manhattan, can be reached by the IRT (Lexington Avenue) subway. Take a local and get off at the 23rd Street Station. It can also be reached by buses on Madison Avenue or Broadway. Open Wednesday through Sunday from 9 A.M. to 5 P.M. Closed all Federal holidays. Admission $1; free for children under 17 and seniors 62 and over. Tel.: (212) 260-1616.

Sagamore Hill is at the end of Sagamore Hill Road, in Cove Neck, Oyster Bay. It can be reached by the Long Island Expressway to Exit 41 North to N.Y. 106 North. This leads directly to Oyster Bay. Turn right at the third traffic light and follow the signs. Open daily from 9:30 A.M. to 5 P.M. Admission $1. Senior citizens (62 and over) and children under 17, free.

THE FOUR-STORY BROWNSTONE stands in what is now a business street, a far cry from the trim and respectable residential neighborhood that saw the birth of Theodore Roosevelt on October 27, 1858. Four years earlier his father, Theodore, Sr., had brought his southern bride, Martha Bulloch Roosevelt, to live in the house at 28 East 20th Street, New York City. Though the house was neither large nor lavish by the standards of the day, it was adequate for a young couple of moderate means. For the next twenty years it was the family's home, and it was here that Theodore's sisters and brother were born: Anna in 1855, Elliot in 1860 and Corinne in 1861.

Roosevelt passed his formative years here. Poor health plagued young Theodore and one of his earliest recollections was of his father walking up and down the room at night holding him in his arms. When he was twelve and his health was beginning to improve, his father spurred him along by installing a gymnasium on the porch off the nursery. "You have the mind, but not the body," his father told him, and he responded by working out on the apparatus along with the rest of the neighborhood youngsters.

The birthplace and early home of Theodore Roosevelt at 28 East 20th Street in New York City. The brownstone still stands in what is now a commercial neighborhood. (Courtesy U.S. National Park Service, Department of the Interior.)

He learned to read at an early age and found special solace in books on natural history. Physically unable to attend school, he extended his uneven tutoring by wide reading. By eight he was a budding naturalist, and by fourteen he had grasped the main tenets of Darwin.

When Theodore was ten the Roosevelts went off to Europe for their first grand tour. Often homesick, ill or exhausted, Theodore later remembered the trip with distaste. Four years later when the family returned to Europe he had better health and more resolve and found the Continent, Egypt and Syria interesting for their birds as well as their monuments. His travels were a broadening influence that helped make up for his lack of systematic schooling before college.

When Mrs. Roosevelt and the children returned to New York in late 1873, they moved into a new home at 57th Street. The birthplace on 20th Street remained in the Roosevelt family until 1899. As the neighborhood passed from residential to commercial use, the house underwent a series of commercial alterations that destroyed the original fabric. In 1919, encouraged by Roosevelt's widow and two sisters, the Women's Roosevelt Memorial Association (which merged with the Theodore Roosevelt Association) raised funds to buy and reconstruct the house. They also bought the adjoining property, the house of Robert Roosevelt, uncle of Theodore. The father of Theodore Roosevelt, Sr., had originally built the two houses for his sons.

The house was originally entered by climbing the stoop over the English basement. On the first floor were a parlor and a library, both opening onto a hall, with a dining room running across the full width of the house at the rear. On the second floor were three bedrooms, and on the third floor, three more, with servants' quarters on the fourth. A door on the second-floor porches connected the two original houses.

"It was furnished," Roosevelt later wrote of the house, "in the canonical taste of New York, a period in which men of substance liked to have their homes reflect the dignity and solidarity of their traditions and their lives. The black haircloth furniture in the dining room scratched the bare legs of the children as they sat on it. The middle room was a library, with tables, chairs and bookcases of gloomy respectability."

A feature of the house was the arrangement of the yard in back. Both houses had wide porches overlooking their yards, and the gardens of the Robert Goelet estate on 19th Street.

In the reconstructed house the living rooms and two bedrooms have been restored to the period of Theodore's boyhood. The drawing room, with its high ceiling, magnificent mirrors, crystal chandelier and blue satin hangings, has the characteristic elegance of the period. The front bedroom, in which Theodore was born in 1858, contains original 1866 furniture and a portrait of his mother. Next to it is the nursery, and beyond that is the open porch which was used as a gymnasium.

Sagamore Hill was built by Theodore Roosevelt during 1884 and 1885 and remained his permanent home for the rest of his life. Following the death of his first wife, Alice Hathaway Lee, only hours after the birth of a daughter, the young Roosevelt moved in with his sister, Anna, and the infant. In December 1886 Roosevelt married Edith Kermit Carow, a childhood friend. The following spring they arrived at Sagamore Hill, and here, except for absences imposed by Theodore's public career, the Roosevelts spent the rest of their lives. Here were born three of their five children: Theodore Jr., Kermit and Ethel. Here to the "Summer White House" came national and international figures from every walk of life. Here on January 6, 1919, Theodore Roosevelt died peacefully in his sleep at the age of sixty, and here Edith Roosevelt lived until her death in 1948 at the age of eighty-seven.

When Theodore was fifteen, his father established the family's summer residence at Oyster Bay, and Theodore spent his summer vacations exploring the fields and

Sagamore Hill in Oyster Bay, Long Island, New York, built by Theodore Roosevelt in 1884–85 and his permanent home for the rest of his life. As President, Roosevelt spent summers here, and the house became known as the "Summer White House." (Courtesy U.S. National Park Service, Department of the Interior.)

woodlands of Cove Neck. Six months after graduating from Harvard in 1880, Roosevelt bought the hill on Cove Neck where his home now stands. A barn was the only building on the tree-barren hill. For this property he paid $10,000 in cash and assumed a twenty-year mortgage for the $20,000 balance. Two other purchases brought the total area to 155 acres, of which he kept 95, selling the rest to an aunt and his older sister.

A New York architectural firm drew up plans for the home, but before the final agreement of its construction was signed, Theodore's wife died, followed by the death of his mother—in the same house and on the same day. Determined to have a suitable home for his infant daughter, he contracted to build for $16,975 the house that was to become known as Sagamore Hill. The name came from the old Sagamore Mohannis, who, as chief of his little tribe (sagamore means chief or wise man), signed away his rights to the land.

In 1889, after a short two years of writing and playing host to scores of visitors attracted to the young squire of Sagamore Hill, Roosevelt was named a member of the U.S. Civil Service Commission, the first major step in a lifetime of distinguished public service.

The 30-by-40-foot Trophy Room or north room, added in 1905 and designed by C. Grant LaFarge. (Courtesy U.S. National Park Service, Department of the Interior.)

All rooms at Sagamore Hill contain items used and loved by the Roosevelt family and which reveal the wide range of Roosevelt's interests. (Courtesy U.S. National Park Service, Department of the Interior.)

Throughout his career—as president of the Police Commission of the City of New York, Assistant Secretary of the Navy, lieutenant colonel of the famed Rough Riders, governor of New York, Vice-President and then President—Sagamore Hill was the house to which he always returned. It was on the wide piazza that Roosevelt was formally notified of his nomination as governor of New York in 1898, as Vice-President in 1900 and as President in 1904.

The piazza at Sagamore Hill, which in Roosevelt's day overlooked Oyster Bay Harbor. (Courtesy U.S. National Park Service, Department of the Interior.)

During the summers of 1901 to 1909, Sagamore Hill was the center of the day-to-day administration of the country's affairs. Reams of copy were filed from there by correspondents who maintained a vigil at the "Summer White House."

Sagamore Hill is a rambling, solidly built, twenty-three-room Victorian structure of frame and brick. It is little changed from the time, a half-century ago, when it was TR's home. On the first floor are a large center hall, the library that served as Roosevelt's private office, the kitchen and the spacious north room added in 1905. This room was designed by Roosevelt's friend, C. Grant LaFarge, son of the artist John LaFarge. The 30-by-40-foot room is built of Philippine and American woods: mahogany, black walnut, swamp cypress and hazel. Crammed with hunting trophies, flags and furniture, the trophy room reflects the interest and spirit of Theodore Roosevelt.

The second floor contains the family bedrooms, the nursery, guest rooms and the room with the great porcelain bathtub. The gun room, housing Roosevelt's collection of hunting arms, is on the top floor. Other rooms include quarters for maids and for a cook, a sewing room, a schoolroom where some of the children were tutored and the bedroom of Theodore Roosevelt, Jr., as it was in his precollege days.

Furnishings throughout the house are original Roosevelt pieces. In every room are items used and loved by the family. On every side are crowded bookshelves, the contents revealing the wide range of Roosevelt's interests. A number of them were written by him (his published works comprise more than two thousand titles dating from 1877 to his death).

On the south and west sides of the house is the spacious piazza from which Roosevelt looked out over Oyster Bay Harbor and Long Island Sound. On the grounds are landscaped gardens and, nearby, the Old Orchard Museum, formerly the home of General Theodore Roosevelt, Jr., containing displays relating to the President and his family.

22

William Howard Taft

THE BIRTHPLACE AND BOYHOOD HOME IN CINCINNATI, OHIO.

WILLIAM HOWARD TAFT, THE twenty-seventh President, was born on September 15, 1857, in a first-floor bedroom of the family home at 2038 Auburn Avenue in Cincinnati. Writing to her sister, Delia Torrey, almost two months later, Louise Taft said, "He is perfectly healthy and hearty and I take real comfort in taking care of him. He is very large for his age, and grows fat every day. The question of complexion is not yet settled—his eyes are at present 'deeply, darkly, beautifully blue.' "

By 1870, when Taft was thirteen, Cincinnati had a population of more than 200,000, scattered along the Ohio River and upon the seven hills that form an arc above the river. The atmosphere was one of many small villages rather than that of a large city. The five Taft boys lived like others of their age: they swam, skated, fought, played baseball. Young William Howard was an avid second baseman and never lost his interest in baseball. He inaugurated the Presidential custom of throwing out the first ball of each new season.

He attended Woodward High School, one of the first public schools to offer college preparation programs. He graduated second in his class in 1874 and left for Yale, where he also graduated second in his class. In 1878, Taft returned home to study law and received a degree from Cincinnati Law School. In June 1886 he married Helen Herron of Cincinnati. They had three children: Robert Alphonso, who became a U.S. senator; Helen Herron; and Charles Phelps II.

Shortly after his twenty-third birthday (1881) Taft became assistant prosecutor for Hamilton County. Subsequently he was appointed collector of internal revenue for Ohio and Kentucky (1882); judge of the Ohio Superior Court for Cincinnati (1887); Solicitor General of the U.S. (1890); U.S. circuit judge for the 56th Judicial District (1892); president of the Philippines Commission (1900); civil governor of the

The birthplace and boyhood home of William Howard Taft in Cincinnati, Ohio. This photo was taken around 1868, and shows the Taft family, including young Will, on the front lawn of the yellow brick house.

Philippines (1901); and Secretary of War (1904). He was elected President of the United States in 1909, appointed Kent professor of constitutional law at Yale University in 1913 and named Chief Justice of the United States in 1921.

Taft was the prominent son of a prominent father. Alphonso Taft had served as Secretary of War and Attorney General under President Ulysses S. Grant. He later went to Vienna as minister to Austria-Hungary, and to St. Petersburg as minister to Russia for President Chester Arthur. Though William Taft himself was thoroughly interested in politics, he was not politically ambitious. His first love was the law. His ambition was always to become a justice of the Supreme Court, an honor he placed even above that of the Presidency.

As President, Taft was responsible for a revised tariff law which secured the protection of American commerce against discriminatory practices by foreign governments and established free trade with the Philippines. In 1909 he proposed the first Federal income tax. In 1912 he urged Congress to adopt an annual Federal budget. He filed more antitrust suits in his four years than any previous administration. He established a Children's Bureau and the Department of Labor. The popular mind saw him as catering to big business. In the 1912 Republican convention he won renomination over Roosevelt. Roosevelt and his progressive followers, claiming foul play, then formed the Bull Moose party, which divided the Republican vote enough for the Democratic candidate, Woodrow Wilson, to win.

After defeat Taft became Kent professor of constitutional law at Yale. During World War I he was named co-chairman of the National War Labor Board. In 1921 President Warren G. Harding named him Chief Justice of the United States, the office Taft had always wanted. He became the only man who served as both President and Chief Justice. He died in Washington on March 8, 1930, and was buried in Arlington National Cemetery.

The William Howard Taft birthplace is a two-story brick home bought in 1851 by Alphonso Taft, who had it extensively remodeled to accommodate a growing family. The home remained in the family until 1899. In 1961 the Taft Memorial Association, under the leadership of Charles Phelps Taft II, son of the President, acquired control of the house and grounds. It was designated as a National Historic Site on December 2, 1969. The home and grounds have been restored by the National Park Service, and the house opened to the public in 1988.

The Tafts liked their new home. It was out of the city with its hot, humid summers and winter smog. The price paid for the house and three acres of land was $10,000. It had a frontage of 100 feet and extended east 769 feet down a steep hill. Within a few weeks after the Tafts moved into the house they contracted to build an addition consisting of a three-story 41-foot-by-23-foot brick ell. In all it was a substantial house with a kitchen, dining room, an observatory positioned on the widow's walk, a large double parlor, a library, and rooms for Will's parents, grandparents, four brothers, sister and three live-in servants.

Today, four restored rooms reflect the Tafts' family life during Will's boyhood years, 1857–74. The remainder of the three-story house is made up of exhibit space that charts the life and career of William Howard Taft.

23

Woodrow Wilson

THE BIRTHPLACE IN STAUNTON, VIRGINIA; THE BOYHOOD
HOME IN COLUMBIA, SOUTH CAROLINA; AND THE
HOUSE IN WASHINGTON, D.C.

HOW TO GET THERE/WHEN TO VISIT

The **Woodrow Wilson Birthplace** is located on North Coalter Street in
Staunton, Virginia, adjacent to Mary Baldwin College. Open to visitors
daily from 9 A.M. to 5 P.M. Closed Thanksgiving Day, Christmas Day and
New Year's Day. Admission $5 for adults, $1 for children 6 to 12; children
under 6, free. Tel.: (703) 885–0897.

The **boyhood home** is located in the center of downtown Columbia at 1705
Hampton Street. Open Tuesdays through Saturdays from 10 A.M. to 4 P.M.
and Sundays from 2 P.M. to 5 P.M. Closed Mondays. Admission, $3 for adults,
$1.50 for students. Senior citizens free in March. Fifty-cent discount to AAA
members. No charge to see grounds.

The **house in Washington** is at 2340 "S" Street, NW, near Dupont Circle,
and can be reached by either Massachusetts or Connecticut Avenue. Open
daily, except Mondays and major holidays, from 10 A.M. to 4 P.M. Admission
is $3.50 for adults and $2 for senior citizens and students. Children under 7
and members of the National Trust for Historic Preservation are admitted
free.

THOMAS WOODROW WILSON, THE twenty-eighth President, was born in the Manse
of the First Presbyterian Church in Staunton, Virginia, on December 28, 1856. The
son of a Presbyterian minister, Wilson studied political science at Davidson and at
Princeton and received a doctorate in the subject in 1886 from The Johns Hopkins
University, Baltimore. From 1885 to 1902, Professor Wilson taught American
history and political science, first at Bryn Mawr, then at Wesleyan University in
Connecticut and, from 1890, at Princeton. He was appointed president of Princeton
in 1902 and served until 1910, when he was elected governor of New Jersey.

On November 4, 1912, Governor Wilson was elected President of the United States. He entered the White House as the heir to the Populist-Bryan tradition, which could be traced to a deeply rooted faith in democracy and humanitarian reform. He set a course termed "The New Freedom," which prompted domestic legislation that resulted in the Federal Reserve Act, the creation of the Federal Trade Commission and passage of the Clayton Anti-Trust Act. As President and a leader in the war-torn world of 1914 to 1919, he dedicated himself to "making the world safe for democracy." To realize this goal, he himself led the American delegation to the Peace Conference at Versailles, where his "Fourteen Points" for peace included "a general association of nations . . ." that gave birth to the League of Nations. With the inauguration of President Warren G. Harding on March 4, 1921, Mr. Wilson retired to a house at 2340 "S" St. in Washington, D.C. He died there on February 3, 1924, and was buried three days later in a crypt at the Washington National Cathedral.

The Reverend Dr. Joseph Ruggles Wilson and his wife, Jessie Woodrow Wilson, moved into the house that was to be Woodrow's birthplace in March of 1855. The Wilsons lived in the Manse in Staunton for almost two and a half years, moving then to Augusta, Georgia, in November 1857, when Dr. Wilson was called to be pastor of the First Presbyterian Church there.

The birthplace is a three-story Greek Revival mansion built in 1846. The house, with exterior brick painted white and a black metal roof, is situated on a hill that permits a full-height basement with two stories above. The East Front (on Coalter Street) has a one-bay classical entrance porch. The interior consists of a central hall with two rooms on each side on all three levels. Each room has a fireplace with plain

The birthplace of Woodrow Wilson in Staunton, Virginia. Shown is the east front of the Manse of the First Presbyterian Church (Wilson's father was the minister there), with the 1919 Pierce-Arrow limousine used by Wilson while President and purchased by him for private use after he retired from office. The Wilsons lived here for two and a half years.

Western façade of the Woodrow Wilson Birthplace in historic Staunton, Virginia, overlooks a terrace boxwood garden. The Greek Revival house was built in 1846 by Staunton's Presbyterian Church as a manse for its minister. The house is handsomely restored to its appearance at the time of President Wilson's birth here in 1856. (Courtesy Woodrow Wilson Birthplace Foundation, Inc.)

mantelpieces and plastered walls either painted various colors or papered, like those in the hall. Most rooms have simple cornices and trim. At the West Front is a two-story portico on a raised pedestal with four large Doric columns. The massive portico looks out upon the church where Woodrow Wilson's father was minister, and on the female seminary, now Mary Baldwin College.

The interior of the Manse mirrors a simple but gracious life-style. The Wilsons organized their homes with a kitchen, servants' quarters, a pantry-storeroom, and a family dining room on the ground level. On the first floor they arranged a bedroom, study, parlor and dining room, and on the second floor a guest bedroom, a bedroom for the two Wilson daughters, a playroom and a storage or trunk room.

Notable family pieces include the Bible that records Thomas Woodrow's birth, portraits of Mr. Wilson's mother and father, musical instruments used by the family, pieces of the Wilson family silver and china, President Wilson's letters and books, and many other mementos associated with Mr. Wilson's tenure at Princeton and as President of the United States. Period furnishings similar to those used by the Wilson family while in residence are also part of the present collection.

Below the west front of the Manse is the 19th-century Victorian town garden dominated by terraced lawn, brick walkways and bow-knot flower beds. Century-old boxwood, shrubs of the 1850s and other period plantings are featured. The garden and lower terrace were built through gifts of The Garden Club of Virginia.

President Wilson's restored Pierce-Arrow limousine is exhibited in the new museum building. The auto was leased by the government in June 1919 for White House use, and President Wilson bought the car in 1921 from the Pierce-Arrow Motor Car Company. He used the limousine until his death.

In 1990 a 13,000-square-foot mansion adjacent to the reception house, having recently been renovated, was opened as a museum. It includes seven galleries of exhibits about Woodrow Wilson's life and times, with photographs from the Birthplace collections and numerous artifacts that are not appropriate to show in a historic house of the 1850s. There are also a library and rooms for school programs.

The Reverend Wilson and family moved into the house in Columbia in 1872, two years after their arrival there. Thomas Woodrow Wilson, called Tommy, their third child and eldest son, wore glasses, liked to read books and was also a good ball player. At sixteen he was tall, lanky and serious-looking.

Those years were the hard times of Reconstruction in post-Civil War South Carolina. Professor Wilson was in relatively comfortable financial circumstances, however, and with some aid from Mrs. Wilson's family was able to build the new house. Besides his professorship at the Theological Seminary one block away, he was minister at the First Presbyterian Church. So there were certain refinements, like gas lighting, the Wilsons were able to afford in this, the only home they ever owned.

The building, though conservative, reflected the era's love for bay windows, arched doorways, and iron mantels painted to look like marble. The colors Jessie Wilson selected, faint traces of which were discovered beneath layers of wallpaper and paint, were typical of her time—pale yellow, mauve, royal blue, burgundy, apple green. The present interiors have been restored to the ambience that the Wilsons and their contemporaries loved.

The present collection of furniture is in some cases actual Wilson furniture, the rest from similar Columbia homes of the period. Sentimental clutter mingles in the rooms together with typical artifacts of the age; the antimacassar, the lambrequin, the ottoman. Outside, tea olives, magnolias and dogwoods grow enormous and gnarled where the Wilsons planted them nearly a century ago.

Left: Main entry hall, Wilson birthplace. (Photo by Dennis Sutton. Courtesy Woodrow Wilson Birthplace Foundation, Inc.) *Right: Room in which Thomas Woodrow Wilson was born on December 28, 1856.* (Photo by Dennis Sutton. Courtesy Woodrow Wilson Birthplace Foundation, Inc.)

Parlor, Wilson birthplace. (Photo by Dennis Sutton. Courtesy Woodrow Wilson Birthplace Foundation, Inc.)

The future President spent part of his teens in this house. At sixteen he joined the Presbyterian Church, an early indication of the religious dedication that remained all his life.

In the autumn of 1875 the Reverend Wilson accepted the ministry of the First Presbyterian Church of Wilmington, North Carolina, moving there with his family on September 25 of that year. Young Thomas Woodrow Wilson never lived in South Carolina again. As President he often reminisced sentimentally about his Columbia home and its part in his life.

On inauguration day, 1921, President and Mrs. Wilson (his second wife, the former Edith Bolling Galt, whom he married in 1915) left the White House for the last time. After attending the ceremonies for President Harding at the Capitol, they drove to their new home on "S" Street.

One of Wilson's unfulfilled ambitions was to build a house from his own plans (a sketch hangs on the wall of his bedroom) but they could not afford it, and Mrs. Wilson spent several weeks looking at available houses in Washington. She chose the red brick Georgian-style house on "S" Street, designed in 1915 by architect Waddy B. Wood for Henry Parker Fairbanks. Mrs. Wilson later described the house as "an unpretentious, comfortable, dignified house, fitted to the needs of a gentleman." She told her husband about her find and was pleasantly surprised when, on their fifth wedding anniversary, he took her to the house and, following a Scottish custom, presented her with a piece of sod from the garden and the key to the front door.

The Wilsons installed an elevator and a billiard room, constructed a brick garage with a large and airy porch over it, and placed iron gates at the entrance to the drive.

In the main stairwell is a painting of an Armenian girl, presented to the President for his efforts to help the suffering Armenian people.

In the drawing room on the second floor hangs a Gobelin tapestry, "The Marriage of Psyche," presented to President and Mrs. Wilson by the French ambassador as a personal gift from the French government. The king and queen of Belgium presented the hand-painted set of eighteen plates; each plate represents a

Boyhood home of Woodrow Wilson in Columbia, South Carolina. The young Wilson lived here for nearly three years, from age sixteen to eighteen. Wilson's father, who was a professor at the local Theological Seminary and a minister at the First Presbyterian Church, had the house built in 1870–72 with gas lighting and other refinements that his comfortable position afforded. (Courtesy Historic Columbia Foundation, Inc.)

historic place in Belgium. The dessert plate on exhibit was one used by James and Dolley Madison in the White House. The portrait of Edith Wilson was one of the first painted of her while she was in the White House. It is by the Swiss artist Müller-Ury. The carved mahogany reading desk and watercolor of the Piazza di Spagna were gifts from the Italian government.

Most of the volumes in the library are either books on the Wilsonian period or biographies of Wilson and his contemporaries. Many of them are specially bound presentation copies and most of them are inscribed. The leather-covered high-back chair was used by the President at Cabinet meetings and presented to him by the Cabinet. Above the mantel is a portrait of Wilson painted by Stanislav Rembski in 1941 from photographs. The twenty-three small pictures on the wall to the right of the mantel are of the Bolling family ancestors. The Bible is the one used by the

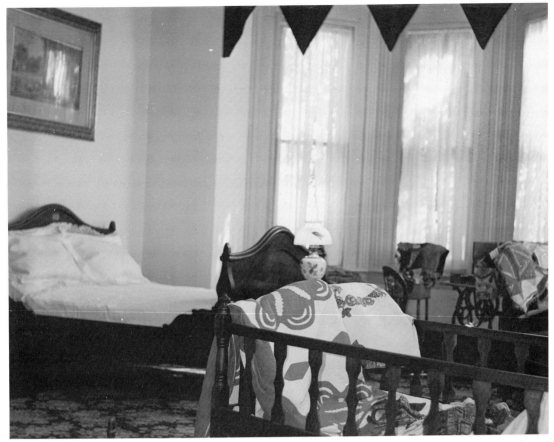

Bedroom with sunny bay window in Wilson's boyhood home at Columbia. The bed in the back left is the bed Woodrow Wilson was born in. (Courtesy Historic Columbia Foundation, Inc.)

Dining room in Wilson boyhood home. The sideboard on the right is a Wilson family piece.

The house on "S" Street in Washington, D.C., where the semi-invalid Wilson lived during the last three years of his life.

President when he took his oath of office as governor of New Jersey and later twice as President of the United States. The pen and penholder were used when he signed a proclamation of a state of war between the United States and Imperial Germany. The silver chest with an illuminated scroll inside was presented by the City of Manchester, England.

President Wilson's bedroom is arranged exactly as it was in the White House. Every article is in the same relative position. Over the extraordinarily large bed hangs a long silk banner that shows the Stars and Stripes flung wide to the breeze. Over the door is the original Red Cross poster called "The Greatest Mother in the World." (A sculpture of the "Mother" is on the second-floor landing.) On the mantel is an empty brass shell that held the first shot fired by the American troops in World War I.

From the time he left the Presidency until his death three years later on February 3, 1924, Wilson lived in the house as a semi-invalid. He could walk only by using a cane and used the elevator to move between floors. Most of his meals were taken on a small table in the library. An occasional drive in Rock Creek Park was one of his few outdoor excursions. He spent most of his time in the library listening to Mrs. Wilson read aloud, looking at illustrated magazines or receiving visitors.

The Georgian-style townhouse is filled with Wilson memorabilia—from his books, typewriter and clothes to World War I souvenirs and the only baseball autographed by a king (King George V). Unlike many other historic sites, the Woodrow Wilson house has the feeling of a comfortable home. Many of the rooms are filled with growing plants. (Mrs. Wilson liked plants.) In the President's bedroom hangs a portrait of actress Jane Russell's mother. He bought it because of its resemblance to his first wife.

During the years the Wilsons lived on "S" Street, most people saw only the outside of the house. They greeted him on Armistice Day 1923, when he made a short speech from the porch, and many were there, kneeling on the sidewalk across the street, the day he died.

Many people saw his death in 1924 as the end of an era. They had found him the public servant who most often expressed for them the hopes and fears they were unable to articulate. Although his strong sense of duty and his concern for justice seemed old-fashioned, he had been one of the first statesmen to realize that the world had become small and that every nation's actions could not be isolated but had international consequences. The nation was turning back to isolationism as a result of the recent war, but Wilson had urged us to live as though we were "all riders on the earth together."

Dining room at the "S" Street house.

Library at "S" Street house. Wilson took most of his meals here.

Wilson's bedroom at "S" Street, with silk banner over bed.

24

Warren Gamaliel Harding

THE HOME IN MARION, OHIO.

HOW TO GET THERE/WHEN TO VISIT

The **Harding home and museum,** administered by The Ohio Historical Society, are located at 380 Mount Vernon Avenue, Marion, Ohio, on State Route 95. From Memorial Day to Labor Day they are open Wednesday through Saturday from 9:30 A.M. to 4:30 P.M. and on Sunday from 12 to 4:30 P.M. Other times in April, May, September and October open by appointment from 9 A.M. to 4 P.M., Monday through Friday. Closed November through March. Admission is $2.50 for adults, $2 for seniors and $1 for children 6 to 12. Special rates available by arrangement for tour groups and school groups. Tel.: (614) 387-9630.

In 1920, A WAR-WEARY and war-sick people, yearning for a healing and strengthening leader in the White House, elected Warren Gamaliel Harding as the twenty-ninth President. He was elected by the largest majority of votes ever received by a Presidential candidate up to that time. The people were anxious to get back into the ways of peace and stay there, to help restore normal operations of business and industry. Harding was known as a calm man who hated strife and discord. He had a friendly and gracious personality, and the people wanted him to restore "normalcy," a word he virtually brought into the language.

He was born November 2, 1865, at Blooming Grove (then Corsica), Morrow County, Ohio. Ancestors on his father's side were Scotch-Irish and on his mother's, Dutch. He was the firstborn of a family of eight. His early education was in the public school at Caledonia, Marion County. Later he attended Ohio Central College at Iberia, earning his way as a laborer. He received his Bachelor of Science degree at Ohio Central and then became a teacher in a one-room schoolhouse, north of Marion. At the age of nineteen he purchased the Marion *Daily Star,* which he published successfully until he sold it in 1923 to a newspaper chain. He was the first journalist to become President.

His political career began on November 6, 1898, when he was elected to the Ohio State Senate. Then followed election as Ohio lieutenant governor on November 3, 1903; defeat as the Republican candidate for governor on November 8, 1910;

Home of Warren G. Harding in Marion, Ohio, built by Harding in 1891, when he was a newspaper publisher, and occupied by the Hardings until 1921, when they left for the White House. Harding campaigned for U.S. senator from the front porch.

election to the U.S. Senate on November 3, 1914; and election to the Presidency on November 2, 1920.

His presidential program had three major aims: world peace, efficient management of government finances, and prosperity for the American people through increased friendliness and cooperation among the various economic and social forces in the country. On November 12, 1921, in response to an invitation from President Harding, representatives from Great Britain, France, Italy and Japan convened in Washington to draw up a limitation of armaments treaty. The conference won worldwide acclaim as the first international disarmament conference of its kind ever held.

In June 1923 President and Mrs. Harding began a political trip across the continent and to Alaska, which ended in his sudden illness and untimely death at San Francisco on August 2, 1923. The funeral train that brought him back to Washington passed through towns and cities where it was viewed by countless thousands of grieving people. Following services in Washington, the funeral train, again viewed by silent throngs, carried his body to his home city of Marion, Ohio, to be placed in a temporary tomb at Marion Cemetery.

Dining room of the Harding home, restored to the way it looked in 1900.

The Harding kitchen.

On December 21, 1927, the bodies of both President and Mrs. Harding were removed to the Harding Memorial, a circular monument of white Georgia marble situated in the midst of ten acres of landscaped grounds on the South Edge of Marion on Route 423.

The Harding home in Marion was built by Warren and Mrs. Harding in 1891 and occupied by them until they left for the White House on March 2, 1921. It is a two-story house with a large open porch topped by a balustrade. It was from this front porch that Harding, then a United States senator, conducted his famous "front porch campaign."

During the winter of 1964–65 the house was restored in detail to its condition at the turn of the century. The original gas-and-electric fixtures were put back in place, and decorations, especially wallpaper, were duplicated in authentic detail. The original furniture and furnishings were returned to their positions in accordance with a chart made at the time they were placed in storage. The result is a 1900 atmosphere of hospitality and gracious living.

At the rear of the Harding home is the Harding museum and administrative office. The building is the old "working press" headquarters from which all Harding campaign news was disseminated. It now contains more than 2,000 mementos, including paintings, manuscripts, the Harding family cradle and sixty-five original cartoons associated with Harding's political life.

25

Calvin Coolidge

THE BIRTHPLACE AND HOMESTEAD IN PLYMOUTH NOTCH, VERMONT.

HOW TO GET THERE/WHEN TO VISIT

Plymouth Notch is on State Highway 100A. The **Coolidge birthplace and homestead** are open from Memorial Day through Columbus Day, daily from 9:30 A.M. to 5:30 P.M. Admission $3.

CALVIN COOLIDGE, THE THIRTIETH President, was born on the fourth of July, 1872, in Plymouth Notch, Vermont. He spent his youth there, no doubt picking up practical Yankee politics from the talk in his father's country store and, later, in town meetings. In 1895 he graduated from Amherst, then worked his way to a law degree, joining a law firm in Northampton, Massachusetts, in 1897.

He became active—and successful—in Massachusetts state politics, serving in the state senate, three terms as lieutenant governor and two terms as governor. He gained national prominence for his firm handling of the Boston police strike in 1919. His declaration that there was "no right to strike against the public safety by anybody, anywhere, anytime" sounds particularly relevant in our time. It was so well received in Coolidge's time that "Silent Cal" won the Vice-Presidential nomination on the Harding ticket in 1920. He assumed the Presidency on Harding's sudden death in 1923 and was elected in his own right in 1924.

His administration was marked by the high water of prosperity of the 1920s. As a believer in classical laissez-faire economics, he just let things happen in an administration noteworthy for its lack of noteworthy accomplishments. In 1928 his famous "I do not choose to run" was accepted, and Herbert Hoover got his party's nod. Coolidge died January 5, 1933, at Northampton.

Until his father, Colonel John Coolidge, purchased the home across the street in 1876, Calvin's birthplace in Plymouth Notch was the Coolidge family home. Through the years alterations and changes were made to the interior and exterior of this building.

In 1968 the State of Vermont acquired the birthplace, together with the Coolidge

The Calvin Coolidge homestead in Plymouth Notch, Vermont, purchased by Coolidge's father in 1876, when Calvin was four. The bay window on the first floor of the house was the site of Coolidge's swearing-in as President upon the death of Harding in 1923. Across the street (not shown) is the house in which Coolidge was born. (Courtesy Vermont Division for Historic Preservation.)

family store. With old photos as a guide, the exterior of the birthplace was restored. The interior of the building, which had been used as a private home when it was acquired by the state, had been completely modernized. However, after detailed studies of the original construction, it was restored to its 1872 appearance. It is now furnished with original artifacts from the Coolidge family.

The Coolidge homestead across the street was, in 1923, the setting for the ceremony that made Mr. Coolidge President. It was here that Mr. Coolidge, as Vice-President, was vacationing when word came of the death of President Harding. In the bay window room on the first floor, at 2:47 on the morning of August 3, Colonel John Coolidge, a notary public, administered to his son, by the light of a kerosene lamp, the oath of office of President of the United States.

Kitchen, Coolidge homestead. (Courtesy Vermont Division for Historic Preservation.)

Dining room. (Courtesy Vermont Division for Historic Preservation.)

Parlor. (Courtesy Vermont Division for Historic Preservation.)

Coolidge's study. (Courtesy Vermont Division for Historic Preservation.)

Coolidge's bedroom at the homestead. (Courtesy Vermont Division for Historic Preservation.)

With the passage of years, that nighttime drama enacted in this Vermont village home has become an interesting historical footnote that continues to draw visitors from all over the world. In 1957, the President's son John Coolidge and his son's wife, Florence, gave to the Vermont Board of Historic Sites this original house complete with all of the furnishings that were there on the night of the inauguration. The board has rearranged passageways throughout the first floor so that visitors may now go through every room and see them in their original settings.

Across from President Coolidge's home is the church he knew as a youth and later as President. South of the village lies the Plymouth Notch Cemetery, where, in the winter of 1933, President Coolidge was laid to rest alongside his son Calvin, Jr., and generations of his family. A plain granite headstone marks the President's grave. Here also his generous wife, Grace Goodhue Coolidge, who died on July 8, 1957, lies buried.

Today the entire village of Plymouth Notch has been preserved and is operated as a historical site by the Vermont Division for Historic Preservation.

26

Herbert Hoover

THE BIRTHPLACE IN WEST BRANCH, IOWA; AND THE BOYHOOD HOME IN NEWBERG, OREGON.

HOW TO GET THERE/WHEN TO VISIT

The Hoover birthplace, at the Herbert Hoover National Historic Site, is on Downey Street in West Branch, less than one mile north of exit 254, Interstate 80. Open from 8 A.M. to 5 P.M. daily. Closed on Thanksgiving, Christmas and New Year's days. Admission $1. Those under 17, over 62 or holding Golden Passports admitted free. Tel.: (319) 643-2541.

The Hoover-Minthorn House Museum is one block south of Highway 99W on River Street in Newberg. Open from 1 to 4 P.M., Wednesday through Sunday, March through November, and Saturdays and Sundays in December and February. Closed January and holidays. Admission for adults is $1.50, seniors $1 and students 50 cents. Tel.: (503) 538-6629.

HERBERT CLARK HOOVER, OUR thirty-first President, was born in a two-room cottage in the village of West Branch, Iowa, on August 10, 1874, the son of Hulda Minthorn Hoover and Jesse Clark Hoover, a Quaker blacksmith. His father died when he was six, his mother when he was nine.

With both parents dead, the little boy went to live with his uncle Allan Hoover on a farm near West Branch. In 1886 he was sent to Newberg, Oregon, to live with his uncle Dr. Henry John Minthorn, a physician and also the superintendent of the Friends Pacific Academy, which Herbert attended. (Mrs. Minthorn was principal of the Academy's grammar school.) Dr. and Mrs. Minthorn had three daughters and a son, but the son had died during the winter of 1883 and the Minthorns, who had known young Herbert in West Branch, asked that he be sent to live with them. So, at the age of ten, Herbert Hoover traveled—with his roll of bedding and a large basket filled with chicken—from West Branch, Iowa, to Newberg, Oregon.

A new world opened up in Newberg for Herbert Hoover in those formative years that had a profound bearing on the rest of his life. He became a regular member of a caring—if stern and undemonstrative—family. Although he may not have enjoyed

The birthplace of Herbert Hoover on Downey Street in West Branch, Iowa. The two-room cottage was built by Hoover's father in 1871, and the family lived here until 1879, when they moved to a larger house on Downey Street. The cottage has been restored to its 1871 appearance by the National Park Service. (Courtesy U.S. National Park Service, Department of the Interior.)

every one of the many tedious chores assigned to him by his rather strict uncle— including sawing, splitting and carrying wood for the three stoves, milking the family cow and caring for the doctor's horses—young Herbert was well looked after and was accepted as an important contributing member of the household.

He went on to receive a degree in geology in 1895 as a member of Stanford University's first four-year graduating class, and then began a career as a mining engineer that took him to Australia, China, Europe and Great Britain. In 1908 he established his own company.

When war broke out in Europe in 1914, he helped create and became the first chairman of the Commission for Relief in Belgium. Called home by President Wilson in 1917 to be food administrator, he increased food production enough to feed our Allies abroad with only voluntary rationing at home. As head of the American Relief Administration, he directed postwar food relief in twenty-one European countries. The program was financed in part by a one-hundred-million-dollar appropriation of the U.S. Congress. He also raised private funds to aid European children. In 1921–23 he organized food and medical relief for 18 million Russians threatened by starvation.

As Secretary of Commerce under Presidents Harding and Coolidge from 1921 to 1928, Hoover worked to increase efficiency in business, set up in-depth studies of the economy and pioneered in efforts to regulate and license commercial radio and aviation. In 1927 he took part in the first long-distance demonstration of television.

Famed as an engineer, humanitarian and administrator, Hoover was nominated for President on the Republican ticket in 1928 and won easily over Democrat Alfred

E. Smith. In the months after his inauguration in March 1929, he was confronted with the great stock-market crash and a banking crisis in Europe, followed by a worldwide depression. With the depression deepening through his administration, he was defeated in his 1932 campaign by Franklin D. Roosevelt.

As a private citizen, Hoover devoted much of his time to the Boys' Clubs of America and to writing. In 1946 President Truman asked him to survey world famine conditions in the wake of World War II. He was then called on to serve as chairman of two commissions set up by Congress, one in 1947 and one in 1953, on reorganization of the executive branch of the government. The Hoover Commissions, as they are known, were responsible for many economies in the Federal government.

Hoover died at ninety in New York City on October 20, 1964, and is buried at the "Overlook," the hillside above his birthplace.

Hoover's birthplace was designated a national historic site on August 12, 1965. The Downey Street neighborhood, now a park closed to traffic, contains three separate areas that together memorialize Hoover's life. The portion of the village of West Branch immediately adjacent to and including the birthplace cottage and blacksmith shop recalls the small, late-19th-century midwestern village from which Hoover came. The Presidential Library, administered by the National Archives and Records Administration, represents his years as a public servant and stands near the historic village. The gravesite is the third area.

The birthplace, built by Jesse Clark Hoover in 1871, is a little two-room cottage, now restored and refurnished. It stands on its original site not far from the creek from which the town drew its name. The Hoovers lived in the house until 1879, when Jesse Hoover sold both the cottage and the blacksmith shop and moved his family into a larger dwelling farther south on Downey Street. When the birthplace cottage was restored to its 1871 appearance in 1939, as much as possible of the original furniture belonging to Jesse and Hulda Hoover was acquired for the house.

Privy and woodpile in a corner of the backyard of the cottage. (Courtesy U.S. National Park Service, Department of the Interior.)

A view down historic Downey Street, now closed to traffic, which re-creates the era of Hoover's birth in rural Iowa in 1874. (Courtesy U.S. National Park Service, Department of the Interior.)

During his years in West Branch, Hoover attended meetings here at the Quaker meetinghouse with his parents. In fact, his mother was a recorded minister of this meeting. Neglected for many years, the meetinghouse was purchased by the people of West Branch in 1964 and presented to the Herbert Hoover Birthplace Foundation. In 1964–65, after being moved to its present location on the east side of Downey Street opposite the Presidential Library and southeast of the birthplace cottage, the meetinghouse was restored to its original appearance.

The blacksmith shop, near the birthplace cottage, is typical of an 1870s blacksmith shop. It houses an extensive collection of contemporary tools and other objects.

The Herbert Hoover Presidential Library faces Downey Street and houses the largest collection of papers accumulated by Hoover during his many years of public service. It also holds his collection of books and objects associated with his long and distinguished career. Many items are on display in exhibit areas. A 180-seat auditorium occupies one wing.

The graves of President and Mrs. Hoover are on a hillside about one quarter of a mile southwest of the birthplace cottage. Landscaping provides a circular setting for the flat, white marble gravestones, with a view down the long mall to the birthplace.

The Minthorn house, the boyhood home of Herbert Hoover in Newberg, Oregon. At the age of ten, both parents dead, Hoover came to live with his uncle, Dr. Henry John Minthorn. Like Hoover's parents, Minthorn was a Quaker. He had lost his own son and was eager to provide a home for the orphaned Herbert. (Photograph by Frank Colcord.)

The Minthorn house, Hoover's boyhood home, was purchased and restored with funds given by friends of President Hoover. It is now known as the Hoover–Minthorn House Museum. The interior of the house required few changes. The major ones were the relocation of the stairway leading to the second floor and the reconstruction of the kitchen, which had been destroyed.

The exterior changes included moving the original woodshed to its original position; rebuilding a back porch, wellhouse, outhouse, picket fences and walks; opening the original front porch, which had been incorporated into the house; and removing a glassed-in cupola atop the house.

The original furniture in President Hoover's bedroom came from the Oregon Historical Society. A duplicate bedroom set, now in Dr. Minthorn's bedroom, was found in a house built in 1881 a few miles away from Newberg. This same house furnished the rag carpets and the old pie closet. The cast-iron stove found in the bedroom of Dr. Minthorn is presumed to be part of the original furnishings. The heating stove in the dining room and the wood-burning cookstove were manufactured in the early eighties. The walls are covered with family pictures.

27

Franklin Delano Roosevelt

THE BIRTHPLACE IN HYDE PARK, NEW YORK;
AND THE VACATION PLACE ON
CAMPOBELLO ISLAND, NEW BRUNSWICK, CANADA.

HOW TO GET THERE/WHEN TO VISIT

The **FDR birthplace** in Hyde Park is about 70 miles north of New York City on New York 9, near Poughkeepsie. The Taconic Parkway is the most direct of the several routes available. Open from April through October seven days a week from 9 A.M. to 5 P.M. From November through March closed Tuesdays and Wednesdays. Admission for adults is $3.50; all under 17 and over 62 admitted free.

Principal access to the **summer cottage** on Campobello Island is the Franklin D. Roosevelt Memorial Bridge at Lubec, Maine. To get to Lubec, take U.S. 1 to State 189. North of the park on Campobello are the villages of Welshpool and Wilson's Beach. The park opens the Saturday prior to Memorial Day (that is, the Saturday following Canada's Victoria Day) and remains open for twenty weeks. Visiting hours are from 9 A.M. to 5 P.M. E.D.T. (10 A.M. to 6 P.M. A.D.T.), seven days a week. No admission charge.

FRANKLIN DELANO ROOSEVELT, OUR thirty-second President, was born in the house at Hyde Park on January 30, 1882, the only child of James and Sara Roosevelt. Here he spent much of his life as a baby, little boy and young man; here he brought his bride, Eleanor, in 1905; here they raised their five children; and from here he began a political career that stretched from the New York State Senate to the White House.

Roosevelt was a state senator from 1911 to 1913, Assistant Secretary of the Navy under Woodrow Wilson from 1913 to 1920, and unsuccessful Vice-Presidential candidate in 1920. In 1921 he contracted poliomyelitis, and during his struggle to conquer the disease he spent much time at Hyde Park and, winters, at Warm Springs, Georgia. Refusing to succumb to his affliction, he reentered politics. He was elected governor of New York in 1928 and 1930 and President of the United

The birthplace and family home of Franklin Delano Roosevelt at Hyde Park, New York. Roosevelt lived most of his life here—as a boy, young man, husband, father and politician. He is buried here in the family rose garden. (Photograph by Fred Van Tassell; courtesy Roosevelt–Vanderbilt National Historic Sites.)

States in 1932. As governor and President he came to Hyde Park as often as he could for respite from the turmoil of public life. On April 15, 1945, three days after his death in Warm Springs, Georgia, he was buried in the family rose garden. Seventeen years later, on November 10, 1962, Mrs. Roosevelt was buried beside him.

The first floor of the house contains his office, used as his "Summer White House." Here on June 20, 1942, the President and Prime Minister Winston Churchill signed the historic agreement that resulted in the world's first atomic bomb. Also from this room, on November 6, 1944, he broadcast his last campaign speech, which led to his fourth term as President.

A few large pieces of furniture dominate the main hall. The walls are covered with pictures, most of them naval prints. Directly to the left of the entrance stands a massive oak wardrobe, and immediately before the door, an 18th-century grandfather clock. James and Sara Roosevelt purchased these pieces in the Netherlands in 1881.

Against the wall, just to the left of the clock, stands a large sideboard that James Roosevelt bought in Italy in 1869. In the southeast corner of the hall is a life-size bronze statue of Franklin D. Roosevelt at the age of twenty-nine, done by Prince Paul Troubetzkoy in 1911. Directly behind the statue is a wall case holding many birds Franklin collected when he was eleven years old.

The south hallway leads past the Snuggery (Mrs. Sara Delano Roosevelt's writing and sitting room) to the living room, which occupies the lower floor of the south wing. In this spacious room the family played, read and entertained. Over the left fireplace is the Gilbert Stuart portrait of Isaac Roosevelt, the President's great-great-grandfather, who was active in the Revolutionary War, a member of the state's constitutional convention, a state senator and a member of the state convention that ratified the Constitution of the United States. Over the right fireplace is a portrait of Franklin's great-grandfather, James Roosevelt, who was a New York City merchant, a state assemblyman, an alderman and the first of the family to settle in Dutchess County in 1819.

Ellen Emmett Rand painted the large portrait of Franklin D. Roosevelt at Hyde Park in 1932. The two high-back leather chairs at the left end of the room were Franklin Roosevelt's when he was governor of New York. He received a chair for each of his two-year terms. He always sat in the one on the left.

The Dresden Room takes its name from the delicately wrought Dresden chandelier and mantel set that James Roosevelt purchased in Germany in 1866. The rug is an Aubusson. Sara Roosevelt chose the floral drapes and matching upholstery in 1939, shortly before the king and queen of England visited here. The dining room was a social center for children and guests. On election night, FDR and his political associates filled this room with smoke as they tallied voting returns.

On the second floor is the boyhood bedroom, used by young Franklin and, later, his sons. The many notables who visited the Roosevelts used the Blue and Morning rooms and the rooms on the river side of the hall. Roosevelt was born in the Blue Room, the master bedroom of the house before its expansion in 1915.

At the end of the hallway, in the stone wing over the living room, is FDR's bedroom, which contains his favorite pictures, naval prints and family photographs. The leash and blanket of the President's dog, Fala, are on the Scottie's own chair. Scattered about are the books and magazines that were here at the time of Roosevelt's last visit in March 1945.

Next to the house is the Franklin D. Roosevelt Library, administered by the National Archives and Record Service. The museum section contains the President's study, his ship models, gifts from foreign rulers and special exhibits about the lives and careers of Franklin and Eleanor Roosevelt.

The central part of the building, the oldest section, dates from the early 1800s. When James Roosevelt bought the house in 1867, it had a clapboard exterior. The main house has undergone many renovations and additions with the passage of years, assuming its present form in 1915. The central part, its clapboards removed, was covered with stucco and fronted by a porch with a sweeping balustrade and a small colonnaded portico. On each end, the Roosevelts added a two-story wing.

The house and grounds were designated a National Historic Site on January 15, 1944, a gift from President Roosevelt. The site then consisted of 33 acres containing the home, outbuildings and the gravesite. It was formally dedicated on the first anniversary of the President's death, on April 12, 1946. It now contains 188 acres.

The 2,600-acre Roosevelt Campobello International Park is a unique example of

The main hall at Hyde Park, showing life-size bronze statue of FDR by Prince Paul Troubetzkoy, and, behind it, a case containing birds collected by Roosevelt when a boy. On the walls are naval prints. (Courtesy Roosevelt–Vanderbilt National Historic Sites.)

The "Snuggery" at Hyde Park, which Mrs. Sara Delano Roosevelt used as a sitting room. (Courtesy Franklin D. Roosevelt Library.)

international cooperation, a joint memorial by Canada and the United States. Here are the cottages and grounds where President Roosevelt vacationed, the waters where he sailed and the woods, bogs and beaches where he tramped and relaxed. From 1883, when he was one year old, until he was stricken by polio in 1921, he spent most of his summers on this rugged and beautiful island just across the Canadian border on Passamaquoddy Bay between Maine and New Brunswick. Here a group of New York and Boston entrepreneurs had purchased a large section of land and promoted it as a summer resort for wealthy Americans. James Roosevelt, Franklin's father, purchased four acres and a partially completed house in 1883. By the summer of 1885 this house was finished and the Roosevelts, James, Sara Delano and young Franklin, became summer residents. The site of that house, known in later years as "Granny's Cottage," is just north of Roosevelt Cottage, which was given to Franklin and Eleanor Roosevelt as a wedding gift.

Franklin Roosevelt, the young father, found that his family enjoyed Campobello immensely, and it became customary for all of them to spend July, August and part of September there. The place quickly became as much a part of the lives of his five children as it had been of his.

In the 1920 elections, with FDR running for Vice-President, the Democratic ticket was defeated. Roosevelt turned to private life, taking over as a vice-president

The Dresden Room at Hyde Park takes its name from the lovely Dresden chandelier. (Courtesy Franklin D. Roosevelt Library.)

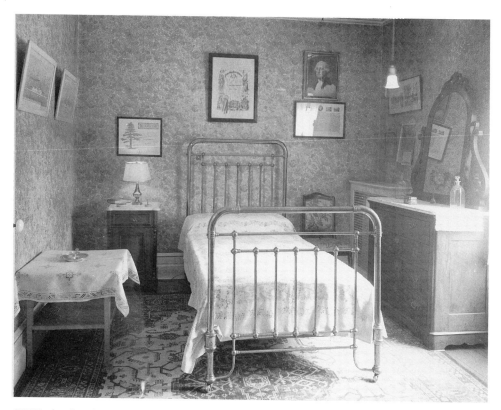

FDR's boyhood room, which was later occupied by his sons. (Courtesy Franklin D. Roosevelt Library.)

FDR's bedroom. Leash and blanket of the President's Scottie, Fala, are on the dog's chair at the foot of the bed. (Courtesy Roosevelt-Vanderbilt National Historic Sites.)

*Portico with colonnade added to the Hyde Park mansion in 1915, together with the two
wings.* (Photograph by Fred Van Tassell; courtesy Roosevelt–Vanderbilt National Historic Sites.)

of the New York office of the Fidelity and Deposit Company of Maryland. By
August, he was looking forward to a good rest on his beloved Campobello. The
family sailed and swam. On August 10 he developed a chill, and the following
morning he was running a high temperature. On August 25 the affliction was
diagnosed as polio.

Nearly twelve years passed before FDR came back to Campobello. Eleanor
Roosevelt and the children continued to visit the island during the summers, but
FDR's convalescence and involvement in active politics prevented his return.

After four years as governor of New York State (1929–1933) FDR was elected
President of the United States. After the first trying one hundred days he felt the
need to go back to Campobello, and sailed the schooner *Amberjack II* from Marion,
Massachusetts. He was at the helm most of the time. He docked on June 30, 1933,
and was greeted by a large crowd, including many friends whom he had known for
years.

He left Campobello for Washington, D.C., on July 1 on the cruiser U.S.S. *Indianapolis*. The visit was too brief for his satisfaction, as were his subsequent visits on July 29–30, 1936, and August 14–15, 1939. His love for the island and his long association with its people left a lasting impression.

It is a short walk from the reception center to Roosevelt Cottage. On view is the room used as an office by President Roosevelt during his 1933 visit, his bedroom, Mrs. Roosevelt's writing room, the living room, dining room, kitchen, laundry, nursery and family bedrooms, including the room where Franklin D. Roosevelt, Jr., was born.

Most of the present furnishings were used by the Roosevelt family. Wallpapers, curtains and rugs are the originals or reproductions provided by the Park Commission. In the rooms are many reminders of FDR and his family: Franklin Roosevelt's crib, the large frame chair used to carry the handicapped President, the family telescope, a collection of canes and a megaphone used for hailing boats and the members of the family. The kitchen, laundry, icehouse, windmill and water tank tell their own stories of life and work in these summer cottages.

In the vicinity of the cottage there are walks through gardens of the Roosevelt area, wooded paths and fields with vistas of sea and land. The International Park has also preserved extensive natural areas that can be hiked or driven through. (A map is available in the brochure distributed free at the Visitor Centre.)

Left: The Franklin D. Roosevelt cottage at Welshpool, Campobello Island, New Brunswick, now an international memorial. The Roosevelt family traditionally spent their summers on Campobello, first in a house known as "Granny's Cottage" and later in the above house, given to Franklin and Eleanor as a wedding gift. (Photograph by Lyman Owen.) Right: The cottage at Campobello in winter.

28

Harry S. Truman

THE BIRTHPLACE IN LAMAR, MISSOURI.

HOW TO GET THERE/WHEN TO VISIT

Lamar can be reached by U.S. 71. The **Truman birthplace** is at Truman Avenue and 11th Street. It is open daily except New Year's Day, Easter, Thanksgiving Day and Christmas Day from 10 A.M. to 4 P.M. On Sundays, it is open from noon to 4 P.M. Admission is free.

THE ANCESTORS OF HARRY S. Truman, our thirty-third President, came to Missouri in 1846 from Shelby County, Kentucky. His grandfather, Anderson S. Truman, settled on a farm in Jackson County. President Truman's father, John, was born on that farm in 1851. John Truman devoted his early years to farming and the raising of livestock in Jackson County. On December 28, 1881, he married Martha Ellen Young. They moved to Lamar, Missouri, where he continued in livestock trading. In 1882, John Truman purchased the birthplace for $685. When Harry S. Truman was one year old, the house was sold and the family moved to a farm at Harrisonville.

The small six-room house is indicative of the modest means of the Truman family in the 1880s. John Truman, like many other Americans of the period, was subjected to the vagaries of an erratic economy. The Truman family knew good times and bad, and the future President grew to manhood with the knowledge that progress is possible only with unremitting struggle. This small cottage typifies the mode of living and home furnishings with which the majority of families lived in the last quarter of the 19th century.

The Truman birthplace was acquired by the United Automobile Workers and donated to the state of Missouri for the creation of a historic site.

The restoration of the house was governed in all aspects by a desire to re-create the atmosphere of the home at the time of President Truman's birth. Many modern aspects of the house were eliminated, such as electricity and heating equipment of too recent a vintage. The structure itself was returned to its 1884 appearance and the house was furnished with period furnishings, wallpapers and carpets. It was dedicated on April 19, 1959.

The birthplace of Harry S. Truman in Lamar, Missouri. The small, six-room house has been restored to re-create the atmosphere of 1884.

The house is now a National Historic Site.

Harry S. Truman was elected Eastern Judge of the Jackson County Court in November 1922, and served as President Judge from 1926 to 1934. He was elected to the U.S. Senate in 1934 and reelected in 1940. On November 7, 1944, he was elected Vice-President of the United States and succeeded to the Presidency on April 12, 1945, upon the death of Franklin D. Roosevelt. He won on his own in 1948. After completing his term on January 20, 1953, Mr. Truman returned to his home in Independence, Missouri, where he died on December 26, 1972.

29

Dwight David Eisenhower

THE BIRTHPLACE IN DENISON, TEXAS;
AND THE BOYHOOD HOME IN ABILENE, KANSAS.

HOW TO GET THERE/WHEN TO VISIT

The **Eisenhower birthplace,** in Denison, Grayson County, can be reached off U.S. 69 and U.S. 75. Open seven days a week 8 A.M. to 5 P.M. from June 1 through Labor Day and 10 A.M. to 12 noon and 1 to 5 P.M. from after Labor Day through May 31. Closed Christmas and New Year's days. Admission for adults and children 12 years and older, $1; children ages 6 to 11, 50 cents; and under 6, free.

The **Eisenhower boyhood home,** part of the Eisenhower Center, is located on S.E. Fourth Street in Abilene, off Kansas Highway 15 (Buckeye Avenue), two miles south of Interstate 70 (Abilene exit). Open 9 A.M. to 4:45 P.M. every day of the year except Thanksgiving, Christmas and New Year's days. No admission charge (admission to nearby Museum $1 for all those 16 years of age and older). Tel.: (913) 263–4751.

NOT UNTIL DWIGHT DAVID Eisenhower was elected President did the modest two-story frame house in Denison, Texas, become known as his birthplace and receive the benefits of restoration. Even Eisenhower himself was not aware that this was indeed where he was born, since he listed Tyler, Texas, as his birthplace when he was a cadet at West Point in 1910.

Eisenhower's father, David J. Eisenhower, was an engine wiper for the Missouri-Kansas-Texas Railroad, which had yards in Denison, the north Texas rail center. The elder Eisenhower changed jobs about a year and a half after his son's birth on October 14, 1890, and in March 1892 the family moved to Abilene, Kansas. Thus the Eisenhower birthplace was virtually forgotten until the thread of a rumor led to the house's discovery, its identity emerging from the pages of Denison's history.

At the end of World War II, Eisenhower's fame was at the crest that carried him into the White House in 1952. Well before that time, rumors were circulating in Denison that the General had been born in that city. Fred Conn, publisher of the

The birthplace of Dwight David Eisenhower in Denison, Texas. Eisenhower's father changed jobs shortly after Ike was born, and the family moved away. The house was not known to be Eisenhower's birthplace until the late 1940s. (Photo by Jimmy VanMeter; courtesy Texas Parks and Wildlife Department.)

Denison *Herald* newspaper, checked an 1891 city directory and found a listing for the Eisenhower family. Conn then located Eisenhower's mother, Mrs. Ida Elizabeth Eisenhower, in Abilene, Kansas, and asked her where Dwight was born. She verified Denison as the birthplace.

By the time Eisenhower was elected President in 1952, a number of committees had organized to make the birthplace a park. In 1953 the Eisenhower Birthplace Foundation, Inc., was chartered to begin the laborious job of research and restoration. The house and property were deeded in 1958 to the State Parks Board, and the National Park Service and the Texas State Parks Board were asked to suggest plans for a park setting about the house. When these plans had been completed, surrounding property needed for park purposes was purchased by the foundation.

The interior of the house contains furniture representative of the 1890s, although a quilt in the bedroom where the President was born is the only authentic Eisenhower possession there. The exterior was also refurbished, and a railed upstairs porch, which had been part of the house when built around 1880, was reconstructed in original form.

President Eisenhower revisited the birthplace several times. Mrs. Mamie Eisenhower accompanied him on the first visit and selected the wallpaper used in the restoration. The birthplace stands at the corner of Lamar Avenue and Day Street. The Katy Railroad cuts across the intersection of these streets at the corner.

Two blocks south of the first Eisenhower home in Abilene is the small frame structure occupied by members of the Eisenhower family from 1898 until 1946. The family purchased the Fourth Street home in 1898 with three acres of land from the President's uncle, Abraham Eisenhower. The original part of the home was built in

Left: The furniture at the birthplace is typical of the 1890s, although not the original family pieces. Right: The kitchen in the Eisenhower birthplace.

The bedroom where Dwight D. Eisenhower was born on October 14, 1890. The handmade quilt at the foot of the bed was made by President Eisenhower's mother. (Courtesy Eisenhower Birthplace State Historic Site and Mrs. Vivian Minor Hassel.)

the late 1880s by Ephraim Ellis, a schoolteacher. The President's grandparents acquired the title in 1892.

The Eisenhower boyhood home is a square, two-story wood-framed structure with a high attic and two chimneys. Attached to the north side of the house is a one-story flat-roofed room. On the west is an L-shaped porch. On the south front, a one-story flat-roof porch extends the entire width of the building. On the three acres were a large barn, chicken house, outhouse and smokehouse, all of which were torn down.

The original first floor consisted of a dining room–kitchen area on the north side, with a coal-burning range, living room, parlor with a bay window, and a hallway running from the southeast corner of the house to the dining room. The original second floor had a north bedroom occupied by the parents and the baby (Earl) and later by Dwight and Edgar. It was called the dormitory because it contained two full-sized beds which four of the boys shared. It had a small bedroom (called the baby room) and a hall running along the east side.

The outside foundation walls were made of native limestone held together with mortar. In the center a basement was dug to house a coal-burning furnace.

Shortly after the family moved into the house, a one-story section was added to the east side and completed in 1900. It included a bedroom for the parents and a small bedroom for the Eisenhower grandfather, Jacob, who lived with the family until his death in 1906. In 1915 a new kitchen and pantry were added.

In 1946, following the death of President Eisenhower's mother, Ida Elizabeth Eisenhower, the home, land and contents of the home were deeded to the Eisenhower Foundation by the sons. The home was to remain exactly as it was when the family lived in it. All the furnishings remain original items, although some pieces have had to be moved because of the need to make space for tours. The furniture is a blend of family heirlooms, antiques and modern pieces.

Eisenhower's boyhood home in Abilene, Kansas, occupied by the family from 1898, when Ike was eight, to 1946. (Courtesy Dwight D. Eisenhower Library.)

The parlor. The furniture, which includes family heirlooms and period antiques, is arranged exactly as it was when the Eisenhowers lived here. (Tourist traffic has forced a slight alteration of this arrangement in recent years.) (Courtesy Dwight D. Eisenhower Library.)

Eisenhower's bedroom, the large "dormitory" on the second floor, which he shared with his brothers. (Courtesy Dwight D. Eisenhower Library.)

30

John F. Kennedy

THE BIRTHPLACE IN BROOKLINE, MASSACHUSETTS.

HOW TO GET THERE/WHEN TO VISIT

The **Kennedy birthplace** is located in Brookline, just outside of Boston. Take the Massachusetts Turnpike (Route 90) to Boston. Get off at Exit 20, Cambridge Street. At the second traffic light turn left into Harvard Street. Turn left onto Beals Street. The site is at number 83 about three-quarters of the way down the block on the right. Open from 10 A.M. to 4:30 P.M. every day of the year except Thanksgiving, Christmas and New Year's days. Admission $1; seniors and children 16 and under free.

JOHN FITZGERALD KENNEDY, THIRTY-FIFTH President, was born in the house at 83 Beals Street in the Boston suburb of Brookline. In 1914 his father, Joseph P. Kennedy, purchased the Beals Street house in anticipation of his marriage to Rose Fitzgerald. They moved into it on returning from their wedding trip. Four of their nine children were born while they lived here: Joseph Jr. (at Hull, Massachusetts) in 1915, John in 1917, Rosemary in 1918 and Kathleen in 1920.

Joseph P. Kennedy, son of a prosperous family from East Boston, was president of the Columbia Trust Company when he and his bride moved to Beals Street. Rose Fitzgerald Kennedy grew up in the world of Boston politics. Through her father, John F. Fitzgerald, onetime mayor of Boston and member of Congress, she had been given opportunities to know leading men and women in all fields and had developed a keen interest in current affairs.

In 1921, when John Kennedy was four years old, the family moved, selling the house to the wife of Edward F. Moore, a close friend and business associate. Since then the house has had various private owners. Three years after the assassination of John F. Kennedy in 1963, it was repurchased by the Kennedy family, with Rose Kennedy supervising the restoration and refurnishing of the house to its 1917 appearance.

The house was designated a National Historic Landmark in May 1965, and two years later included in the National Park System and made a National Historic Site.

It is a three-story house, typical of the pre–World War I period. On the lower floor are the kitchen, dining room, living room and center hall. The living room was the

The birthplace of John F. Kennedy at 83 Beals Street, Brookline, Massachusetts. The Joseph Kennedy family lived here for seven years, moving out when JFK was four years old.

center of the social and recreational life of the family. Many of the objects in this room were used by the Kennedys from 1914 to 1921. The piano was given to Mrs. Kennedy as a wedding present. The mahogany gateleg table stands in its original position, as do the mantel vases over the gas-log fireplace.

The second floor contains a guest room, nursery, study, bath and master bedroom. John F. Kennedy was born in the master bedroom on May 29, 1917. The room is arranged the way it was on that sunny day. The beds, dresser, mirror and night table were in the house originally. Most of the silver toilet articles on the dresser and the chest of drawers belonged to the family, as did the silver vase on the vanity. There are pictures of Mr. and Mrs. Joseph Kennedy and the Kennedy children—Joseph Jr., John, Rosemary and Kathleen.

Most houses did not have multiple bathrooms in the early part of this century, so the bathroom was shared by all members of the family.

With the birth of Joseph Jr. in 1915, his room became the nursery and was used as such during the remainder of the family's years here. After John was born in 1917, the brothers shared the room. With the arrival of Rosemary in 1918, the boys were moved to other quarters, and the room again became a nursery. The bassinet was used for all the newborn Kennedy children. In later years it also sheltered many visiting grandchildren. Originally it had a canopy. In this room are the christening dress, bonnet and outer coat and cape worn by all the Kennedy children and by John F. Kennedy, Jr., son of the President. The book *King Arthur's Knights,* on the chair, was one of the childhood favorites of the President.

Before Rosemary was born in 1918, the guest room was used by visiting family and school friends. After her birth, it was made into a children's room. It is now furnished again as a guest room. The dresser and the bed footboard are pieces originally in the room. The headboard is a reproduction. The silver vase and bud vase on the dresser were wedding gifts. The silver toilet set is marked with Rose Kennedy's initials.

The study was used by Rose Kennedy to write letters, read and do the endless sewing and mending needed by a growing family. The mahogany desk and Martha Washington sewing cabinet were originally in the room. Above the desk is a framed Mother's Day poem given to Rose Kennedy by her children. There are family photographs on the wall.

The Kennedy children did not sit at the large dining-room table with their parents. When they became old enough to manage mealtimes for themselves, they were seated at the small table nearby. The dining room was the scene of several birthday parties for the children. The dining-room furniture, with the exception of the china cabinet, is the same as the Kennedys had at the time. The porringers, napkin rings, forks and spoons on the childrens' table are those used by Joseph Jr. and John and are marked with their initials. All the other china, crystal and silver also belonged to the family. The cut-glass water pitcher and the ruby cut-glass decanter and wine glasses were made in Prague and inherited by Mrs. Kennedy from her mother. In the china cabinet are six tea cups and saucers from the service of Sir Thomas Lipton's yacht *Erin.* Sir Thomas gave them to Rose Kennedy before her marriage.

The kitchen was the domain of the cook and nursemaid. Here, meals were prepared, bread baked, dishes washed and bottles sterilized on the stove for the infants. The nurse and cook, who took their meals there, had their rooms on the third floor. These are now the site's administrative offices.

Nearby, the house on the northeast corner of Abbottsford and Naples Roads is the one the Kennedy family moved into in 1921, when they outgrew the Beals Street residence. John F. Kennedy lived here from the age of four to ten until in 1927 they moved to Riverdale, New York. The Abbottsford and Naples Roads residence is now privately owned and may not be visited.

31

Lyndon B. Johnson

THE BIRTHPLACE IN GILLESPIE COUNTY, TEXAS; AND THE BOYHOOD HOME IN JOHNSON CITY, TEXAS.

HOW TO GET THERE/WHEN TO VISIT

The **Johnson birthplace** in the Texas Hill Country of Gillespie County is located near the LBJ Ranch in Lyndon B. Johnson National Historical Park, 14 miles west of Johnson City and 64 miles west of Austin. The birthplace may be seen as part of the LBJ Ranch bus tour. These tours begin from the Visitor Center of the adjoining Lyndon B. Johnson State Historical Park, right on U.S. 290. Tours are operated from 10 A.M. to 4 P.M. all year round and are free. Tel.: (512) 868-7128. Group reservations: (512) 644-2241.

The **boyhood home,** also part of the Lyndon B. Johnson National Historical Park, is located on 9th Street between "F" and "G" Streets in Johnson City, one block south of U.S. 290 and 50 miles west of Austin. It is open from 9 A.M. to 5 P.M., year-round. From the Visitor Center across "G" Street a walking trail leads to the Johnson Settlement, which includes the restored log cabin of the President's grandfather, as well as other historic buildings and exhibits. No admission charges. Tel.: (512) 868-7128. Group reservations: (512) 644-2241.

AT THE BIRTH OF Lyndon Baines Johnson on August 27, 1908, to young Texas legislator Sam Ealy Johnson, Jr., and his wife, Rebekah, the baby's grandfather proudly announced that "I have a mighty fine grandson, smart as you find them. I expect him to be a United States senator before he is forty." This prediction missed by only four and a half months. Lyndon Johnson became forty on August 27, 1948, and took his seat in the Senate on January 3, 1949. He surpassed even his grandfather's expectations when he became Vice-President in 1961 and the nation's thirty-sixth President on November 22, 1963.

Johnson had taught school for two years when, in November 1931, Richard K. Kleberg, one of the owners of the King Ranch, won a seat in the House of Representatives in a special election. Johnson had worked hard in the campaign, and Kleberg asked him to go to Washington with him as his secretary. It was then that he began learning the intricacies of national politics and found the atmosphere to his liking. During a return trip to Texas in September 1934 he met an east Texas businessman's daughter, Claudia Alta Taylor, known as Lady Bird. On November 17, 1934, they were married.

The birthplace of Lyndon Baines Johnson in Gillespie County, Texas. (National Park Service photograph by Jane Kolter.)

In 1935 Johnson returned to Texas as state director of the National Youth Administration. Under his leadership, programs were developed that aided the state and benefited its youth during the depression. The young people were put to work building roadside parks, repairing school buildings and learning trade skills. More than 75,000 students were able to continue in Texas colleges because of NYA assistance.

In early 1937, Representative John P. Buchanan died. Johnson announced his candidacy for the special election to fill the seat. He campaigned as a strong supporter of President Franklin Delano Roosevelt, and won. In 1941 he ran for the Senate seat vacated by the death of Morris Sheppard and lost to former Texas Governor W. Lee O'Daniel—the only race Johnson ever lost in his political career. He tried again and was elected to the Senate in 1948. He became Democratic Whip in 1951, Minority Leader in 1953 and Majority Leader in 1955. He was elected Vice-President in 1960 as the running mate of John F. Kennedy. The assassination of President Kennedy on November 22, 1963, brought Johnson to the Presidency.

The American electorate in November 1964 gave him a full four-year term with the largest percentage of the popular vote ever received. During his administration, three major civil-rights bills were passed, Medicare began and Federal aid to education grew rapidly. In March 1968 he announced that he would not run for reelection, and in January 1969, he returned to his home in Texas.

The birthplace is a small, two-bedroom farmhouse, about one-half mile east of the LBJ Ranch. It is typical of the homes built in the late 1800s and early 1900s in this region of Texas. In January of 1964, the Johnsons asked Austin architect J. Roy White "to begin a modest restoration of the Samuel Ealy Johnson farmhouse," and by the end of August 1964 the reconstruction of the President's birthplace had been completed. As much as possible, the original materials were used in the reconstruction.

From 1965 through 1969 residents of the area served as volunteer hosts and hostesses, giving guided tours through the birthplace. On December 2, 1969, the 89th Congress passed a bill establishing the Lyndon B. Johnson National Historic Site. On January 15, 1970, the Johnson City Foundation deeded to the United States the birthplace and boyhood home and the acreage on which they stood. In 1980, these areas, administered by the National Park Service, became the Lyndon B. Johnson National Historical Park, managed in cooperation with the adjoining Lyndon B. Johnson State Historical Park.

The boyhood home had been extensively remodeled in 1964. It was restored to the period of 1922 to 1925. The house was again roofed with red cedar shingles. The studs and sheet rock were removed from the one-story Victorian frame house. The sitting area fronting the east porch was rebuilt. The two hall walls which had been removed were replaced. The walls that had been altered in the west wing were replaced. The original wallpaper was reproduced by the roller process. As much of the original pine flooring and beaded ceiling wood as possible was retained. Damaged areas were replaced with similar wood from another structure of the same period. Many of the original doors remain. The fireplace mantels were reproductions. The wash shed and smokehouse south of the boyhood home and the privy were reconstructed of used lumber. The barn was moved to the site from a nearby farm. The birthplace and boyhood home have been refurnished with many pieces of furniture belonging to Rebekah and Sam Ealy Johnson, Jr., and with other Johnson family heirlooms. Other furnishings representative of the period were purchased for the house.

The boyhood home of LBJ in Johnson City, Texas, restored to the period of 1922 to 1925, when Johnson lived here. (National Park Service photograph by Jane Kolter.)

32

Richard M. Nixon

THE BIRTHPLACE IN YORBA LINDA, CALIFORNIA.

HOW TO GET THERE/WHEN TO VISIT

The **Nixon birthplace** is part of The Richard Nixon Library & Birthplace at 18001 Yorba Linda Boulevard, Yorba Linda, Orange County, California. Yorba Linda Boulevard can be reached by exiting east from Highway 57 when traveling either from Los Angeles or San Diego. The birthplace is also served by the Orange County bus system. Open at least from 10 A.M. to 5 P.M. Monday through Saturday and 11 A.M. to 5 P.M. Sundays. Closed Thanksgiving, Christmas and New Year's days. Telephone to confirm operating hours, which are subject to seasonal change. Tel.: (714) 993-3393.

RICHARD MILHOUS NIXON, THIRTY-SEVENTH President of the United States, was born to Francis A. and Hannah Milhous Nixon on January 9, 1913, in a modest frame house built by his father and set among the citrus groves of southern California. Young Richard lived there until he was nine, then moved with his family to nearby Whittier. He graduated from Whittier College in 1934 and then in 1937 from the law school of Duke University in North Carolina. He married Thelma Catherine Patricia ("Pat") Ryan in 1940. During World War II he served as a Naval officer. After his discharge in 1946 he was elected to the U.S. House of Representatives. He was reelected in 1948, and then elected to the U.S. Senate in 1950. He then served as Vice-President in the Eisenhower administration, from 1953 to 1961. Nixon ran for President in 1960 but lost to John F. Kennedy. He likewise lost the California gubernatorial race in 1962. After that he moved to New York and entered the private practice of law, but in a few years reentered politics and was elected President in 1968. In 1972 he was reelected, enjoying an enormous landslide victory over Senator George McGovern. In that year Richard Nixon became the first U.S. President to visit the People's Republic of China, reopening official communication with that nation. He was also the first U.S. President to visit Moscow (in May 1972). On August 8, 1974, plagued by problems deriving from the Watergate scandal, Mr. Nixon announced his resignation, cutting short his second term. At this writing, he and his wife are living in Upper Saddle River, New Jersey.

On July 19, 1990, The Richard Nixon Library & Birthplace in Yorba Linda was officially dedicated by President Bush and former Presidents Nixon, Ford and Reagan. Besides the original birthplace, the privately funded museum and library include a 52,000-square-foot main gallery, a seventy-five-seat amphitheater, a thirty-by-twenty-foot reflecting pool and the First Lady's Garden. The archives (not yet open at this writing) contain the most complete collection anywhere of records of President Nixon's career. The birthplace itself, standing in its original location, has been restored to its appearance in the President's childhood. It includes original furnishings, among them the piano that Nixon learned to play as a boy. In an audio program the former President himself narrates the story of his early life.

The birthplace of Richard M. Nixon in Yorba Linda, California. (Courtesy The Richard Nixon Library & Birthplace.)

33

Gerald R. Ford

THE HOME IN ALEXANDRIA, VIRGINIA.

The **Gerald R. Ford, Jr., house** on Crown View drive, Alexandria, is privately owned and not open to the public.

Born Leslie Lynch King, Jr., in Omaha, Nebraska, on July 14, 1913, Gerald Ford was the son of Leslie Lynch King and Dorothy Gardner King. Two weeks after his birth his parents separated and his mother took him to Grand Rapids, Michigan, to live with her parents. Two years later, after her divorce, Dorothy King married Gerald Rudolph Ford. The Fords began calling their son Gerald R. Ford, Jr., and his name was legally changed in 1935.

Gerald Ford attended high school in Grand Rapids and from 1931 to 1935 attended the University of Michigan at Ann Arbor, where he majored in economics and political science. He also played on the university's national championship football teams in 1932 and 1933. He graduated with a B.A. degree in 1935. In the spring of 1938 he entered Yale Law School, earning his LL.B. in 1941 and graduating in the top twenty-five percent of his class.

He returned to Michigan, was admitted to the bar and set up a law partnership in Grand Rapids. In the spring of 1943 he began service as an officer on the light aircraft carrier U.S.S. *Monterey,* which took part in most of the major operations in the South Pacific. He was discharged as a lieutenant commander in February 1946. In 1948 he married Elizabeth Anne ("Betty") Bloomer. They have three sons and a daughter.

Gerald Ford was elected as a Republican to the House of Representatives in 1948. He was reelected twelve times, serving there until 1973. In 1963 President Lyndon B. Johnson appointed him to the Warren Commission investigating the assassination of President Kennedy. In 1965 Ford became minority leader of the House. When Spiro T. Agnew resigned the office of Vice-President late in 1973, President Nixon chose Ford, a loyal supporter for many years, as the new Vice-President. After the Watergate scandal, Nixon became the first President in U.S. history to resign, and on August 9, 1974, Gerald R. Ford took the oath of office as thirty-eighth President of the United States.

President Ford inherited an administration plagued by war, inflation, fears of energy shortages, and an increasingly assertive Congress. On two separate trips to

The Gerald R. Ford home in Alexandria, Virginia.

California in September 1975, he was the target of assassination attempts. During the 1976 campaign, Ford fought off a strong challenge by Ronald Reagan to gain the Republican nomination. He lost to Jimmy Carter in one of the closest Presidential elections in history.

During most of Ford's twenty-five-year tenure as a congressman from Grand Rapids, during his Vice-Presidency and for the first ten days of his Presidency in August 1974, the Ford family lived in Alexandria, Virginia, in a typical upper-middle-class residence in this Washington, D.C., suburb. The seven-room house consists of a two-story main section, a two-story extension at the east side built to house a garage and the master bedroom, and a one-story extension at the rear. When the Fords moved into it in 1955, theirs was only the second house on the block. The Fords themselves arranged for its construction and reviewed the floor plans. Mrs. Ford planned most of the landscaping. When Mr. Ford became Vice-President, the Secret Service installed a "Command Post" in the garage and made a number of related changes.

Although the house was awarded National Historic Landmark status on December 17, 1985, it remains in private ownership and closed to the public.

34

Jimmy Carter

THE BOYHOOD HOME AT ARCHERY, GEORGIA; AND THE FAMILY HOME IN PLAINS, GEORGIA.

HOW TO GET THERE/WHEN TO VISIT

The **boyhood home** at Archery and the **family home** in Plains are both part of the Jimmy Carter National Historic Site, located ten miles west of Americus, Georgia, on U.S. 280. The homes are at present closed to the public, but the old railroad depot in downtown Plains, which serves as the Site's Visitor Center, contains a small museum. Open daily from 9 A.M. to 5 P.M. Closed Christmas Day. No admission charge. Tel.: (912) 824-3413.

JAMES EARL CARTER, JR., better known as "Jimmy," was born in Plains, Georgia, on October 1, 1924, and grew up on a farm three miles outside of Plains. His father, James Earl Carter, Sr., was a farmer and storekeeper. His mother, "Miss Lillian" Gordy Carter, was a registered nurse. They raised their eldest child Jimmy, their two daughters Ruth and Gloria, and their youngest child Billy to take responsibility for family and farm chores, to respect education, and to be examples to others for their selfless community service.

After graduating from Plains High School in 1941, Jimmy Carter spent one year at Georgia Southwestern College in Americus and another at Georgia Institute of Technology in Atlanta while awaiting his admission to the U.S. Naval Academy at Annapolis, Maryland. After graduating from the Academy in the summer of 1946, he married Rosalynn Smith, also from Plains. For the next seven years the Carter family was stationed in various ports where Mr. Carter served as a naval officer and nuclear physicist. During this time their three sons, Jack, Chip and Jeff, were born.

In 1953 James Earl Carter, Sr., died, and Jimmy Carter decided to resign from his naval career and return to Plains to help the family with their peanut farm and family business, a farmers' supply store. After his return to Plains, he began to help the local community by service to the church, board of education and planning commissions.

Jimmy Carter's political career began in 1963, when he served for two years as a state senator. His first bid for governor of Georgia in 1966 ended in defeat to Lester

The Carter boyhood home at Archery. The barn-like structure in the background is the old commissary where foodstuffs and dry goods were offered for sale to local tenant farmers.

Maddox, but he ran again in 1971 and won. By this time, a daughter, Amy, had been born to the Carters.

While serving his four-year term as governor, Carter began to prepare to campaign for the Presidency in 1975. His success led to his inauguration in 1977 as the thirty-ninth President of the United States, the first to be elected from Georgia.

The Carter boyhood home, constructed around 1918 in the old community of Archery, is a white weatherboard farmhouse with a rectangular shape and hipped roof with a shed dormer in the front. Two interior rock chimneys provide double fireplaces. An open porch with four square wooden posts reaches across the front.

Gabled protrusions at both sides of the house are typical for such houses of the early twentieth century. A central door opens from the front porch into the living room and, from there, a hall takes one to the rear of the house. Three bedrooms are on the east side of the house and a dining room, breakfast room and kitchen on the west side behind the living room.

The four front rooms were originally heated by fireplaces and the kitchen by a wood stove standing in the middle of the room. Jimmy Carter's bedroom was a small room across the hall from the kitchen at the northeast corner. It had no heat. His parents had the middle room and the girls slept in the front bedroom. At the rear of the house was a small porch on which there was a water pump. Until 1937 there was no indoor plumbing or electricity. The ceilings throughout the house were high. On either side of the hearth in the dining room were small anterooms that held books and games. The family moved into Plains in 1949 while Mr. Carter was in the Navy.

The Carter family home on Woodland Drive in Plains.

The present home of the Carter family on Woodland Drive in Plains was constructed in 1961. It is a one-story brick ranch-style home of functional design. The living room, dining room and four bedrooms face the front with its traditional exterior of double front doors balanced on each side by windows reaching down to the floor. Behind the living room, a paneled family room with high ceiling opens onto a small patio at the rear of the house. The patio and rear of the house are of contemporary design. Privacy is provided in this open area by a board-and-batten wall on the south side. The roof is gabled and the central chimney provides two fireplaces. At the southwest corner of the residence is a study designed to hold memorabilia from the Carter term as governor of Georgia.

This home became the residence of the Carter family in 1962, at the beginning of Jimmy Carter's era of public service, when he ran for the state senate. It remained in use as the family home through his terms as state senator, governor and President, when it was used as a retreat from the White House. This is the only home that Mr. Carter has owned.

At present, no admission is granted to the public to either the family home—closely guarded by the U.S. Secret Service—or the boyhood home, which remains in private hands at this writing. It is expected, however, that the latter will soon be acquired by the National Park Service and opened to the public. Meanwhile tourists are invited to stop at the Visitor Center, located in the old railroad depot, the oldest building in Plains, built in 1888, which contains a small Carter museum.

35

Ronald Reagan

THE RANCH IN SANTA BARBARA COUNTY, CALIFORNIA.

Rancho del Cielo is located about twenty miles north of Santa Barbara in the Santa Ynez Mountains, Santa Barbara County, California. It is not open to the public.

RONALD WILSON REAGAN WAS born in Tampico, Illinois, on February 6, 1911, the son of Nellie Wilson Reagan and John Reagan. Educated in Illinois public schools, Ronald graduated from Eureka College in Illinois in 1932 with a degree in economics and sociology. Following a successful but brief career as a radio sportscaster, the future President moved to California to work in motion pictures. His film career was interrupted by three years of service in the Army Air Corps during World War II, but eventually encompassed fifty-three feature-length motion pictures. He also served six terms as president of the Screen Actors Guild and two terms as president of the Motion Picture Industry Council.

In 1952 Ronald Reagan married Nancy Davis. They have two grown children, Patricia Ann and Ronald Prescott. Mr. Reagan also has two other children by a previous marriage, Maureen and Michael (adopted).

From motion pictures Reagan went into television. In the 1950s he was production supervisor and host of *General Electric Theatre*. In 1964–65 he was host of the television series *Death Valley Days*.

The beginning of his public service career came in 1966, when he was elected governor of California. He was chairman of the Republican Governors Association in 1969 and was reelected governor of California in 1970. After completing his second term, Reagan began a nationally syndicated radio commentary program and newspaper column. In 1974–75 he served as a member of the Presidential Commission investigating the CIA.

In November 1975 he announced his candidacy for the 1976 Presidential nomination. He lost narrowly but campaigned vigorously for the Republican ticket and for local candidates in 1976. After the election he renewed his radio commentary program, newspaper column and national speaking agenda. He became a member of the Board of Directors of the Committee on the Present Danger

The adobe house at Rancho del Cielo, Santa Barbara County, California. (Official White House photograph.)

and founded the Citizens for the Republic. In the 1978 election he campaigned on behalf of eighty-six candidates.

In November 1979 Mr. Reagan announced his candidacy for the GOP Presidential nomination. He was unanimously nominated on the first ballot at the Republican National Convention in July 1980. In November he was elected, and on January 20, 1981, Ronald Reagan was sworn in as the fortieth President of the United States.

In August 1984 he was once again the unanimous choice of the Republican Party. He was reelected in November of that year and was sworn in for a second term at the fiftieth Presidential inauguration in January 1985.

The home of Mr. and Mrs. Reagan is at Rancho del Cielo ("Ranch of the Sky") in the Santa Ynez Mountains twenty miles north of Santa Barbara in Santa Barbara County. Overlooking the Pacific Ocean to the west and the Santa Ynez Valley to the east, this sprawling property covers 688 acres and includes a five-room Spanish-style adobe house, a small stable for horses and a manmade pond. A private residence, it is not open to the public.

36

George Bush

The summer home at Kennebunkport, Maine.

> The **Bush summer residence** is located on the water at Walker's Point, Kennebunkport. It is not open to the public.

George Herbert Walker Bush was born to Prescott and Dorothy Bush in Milton, Massachusetts, on June 12, 1924. He graduated from Phillips Academy in Andover, Massachusetts in June 1942 and immediately enlisted in the Navy. He received his commission and wings in 1943 and at the age of eighteen became the youngest pilot in the U.S. Navy. On active duty from August 1942 to September 1945, Bush flew fifty-eight missions against the Japanese in the Pacific theater, earning the Distinguished Flying Cross and three air medals. On January 6, 1945, he married Barbara Pierce of Rye, New York; together they have had six children (one died in childhood). After World War II, George Bush entered Yale University. He completed his economics studies in 1948 as a member of Phi Beta Kappa.

After his graduation, the Bushes took up residence in Texas, where Mr. Bush worked in the oil industry, cofounding three oil companies in the next few years.

His political career began with his election to the U.S. House of Representatives in 1966, representing the seventh district of Texas. He served on the Ways and Means Committee and was reelected without opposition two years later.

From 1971 to January 1973 Mr. Bush served as the U.S. Ambassador to the United Nations and from then to September 1974 as Chairman of the Republican National Committee. In October 1974 he traveled to Peking and served for more than a year as Chief of the U.S. Liaison Office in the People's Republic of China. In 1976 he was Director of the Central Intelligence Agency, and in 1980 he was selected by Ronald Reagan as his running mate. He served two terms as Vice-President under President Reagan before being elected President himself. In January 1989, George Bush was inaugurated as the forty-first President of the United States.

The Bush summer residence at Walker's Point, Kennebunkport, Maine, is an old family retreat built by the President's maternal grandfather, George Herbert Walker, in 1905. Mr. Bush has spent almost every summer of his life there. The rambling, substantial dwelling is perched on a small, rocky strip of land surrounded by the ocean. Damaged by a storm in 1978, the house was later restored. It is now closely guarded by the Secret Service and is closed to the public.

The Bush summer home at Walker's Point, Kennebunkport, Maine. (Photo by David Valdez; official White House photograph.)

Index